Southern Living®
Busy Moms
Weeknight
Favorites

Southern Living®

Busy Moms
Weeknight
Favorites

Compiled and Edited by
Elizabeth Taliaferro

Oxmoor
House®

©2006 by Oxmoor House, Inc.
Book Division of Southern Progress Corporation
P. O. Box 2262, Birmingham, Alabama 35201-2262

Southern Living ® is a federally registered trademark belonging
to Southern Living, Inc.

ISBN-13: 978-0-8487-3128-1
ISBN-10: 0-8487-3128-X
Library of Congress Control Number: 2006933872
Printed in the United States of America
First Printing 2006

Editor in Chief: Nancy Fitzpatrick Wyatt
Executive Editor: Susan Carlisle Payne
Copy Chief: Allison Long Lowery

Busy Moms' Weeknight Favorites

Editor:	Elizabeth Taliaferro
Copy Editor:	Donna Baldone
Editorial Assistant:	Rachel Quinlivan, R.D.
Senior Designer:	Emily Albright Parrish
Photography Director:	Jim Bathie
Senior Photographers:	Ralph Anderson, Randy Mayor, John O'Hagan
Photographers:	Tina Cornett, William Dickey, Beth Dreiling
Senior Photo Stylists:	Kay E. Clarke, Buffy Hargett
Photo Stylists:	Cindy Manning Barr, Katherine Eckert, Jan Gautro, Rose Nguyen, Cari South
Director, Test Kitchens:	Elizabeth Tyler Austin
Assistant Director, Test Kitchens:	Julie Christopher
Food Stylists:	Lyda Burnette, Rebecca Kracke Gordon, Kellie Gerber Kelley, Vanessa McNeil Rocchio, James Schend, Kelley Self Wilton
Test Kitchens Staff:	Kathleen Royal Phillips, Catherine Crowell Steele, Ashley T. Strickland
Director of Production:	Laura Lockhart
Production Manager:	Terri Beste
Production Assistant:	Faye Porter Bonner

Contributors

Indexer:	Mary Ann Laurens
Interns:	Jill Baughman, Ashley Leath, Caroline Markunas, Mary Katherine Pappas, Lucas Whittington
Photographers:	Beau Gustafson, Lee Harrelson, Becky Luigart-Stayner
Photo Stylists:	Melanie J. Clarke, Lydia DeGares-Pursell

Cover:	Mexican Lime-Chicken Soup (page 114)
Back Cover:	Crunchy Ranch Tortilla Chicken (page 132) Chicken Thighs with Thyme and Lemon (page 188)

About Our Nutritional Analysis

- If a recipe has a range of amounts for an ingredient, we analyze with the first amount.

- Garnishes, accompaniments, and optional ingredients are not included in the nutrient analyses.

- When a recipe says to cook pasta according to package directions, we analyzed adding 1 Tbsp. salt to the water per 16 oz. pasta.

- When a recipe calls for hot cooked rice, we analyzed using no added salt for the preparation of the rice.

- We consider a meatless main dish to have 10 or more grams protein per serving.

To order additional publications,
call 1-800-765-6400.

For more books to enrich your life, visit
oxmoorhouse.com

Pork Loin Chops with
Cinnamon Apples **34**

Pork Lettuce
Wraps **152**

Crisp Garlic
Chicken **220**

Santa Fe **232**
Pizza

contents

Family Favorites   14

Recipes sure to make your family happy.

Make-Ahead Meals   96

Make cooking count with these recipes that work
overtime so you don't have to.

Quick Cooking   170

These superfast recipes cook up in record time on the
grill, in the skillet, or in the oven.

Great New Flavors   228

For families with adventurous palates or moms who
want to introduce deliciously daring new dishes.

From One Mom to Another...

Every mom knows the challenge of preparing satisfying meals for her family. I confess I'm no exception. Even as a food professional, juggling work and family life often leads me to ask the same questions you do. *"What's for supper tonight and how am I going to find the time to prepare it?"*

Now, when I was a kid, my mom set a high standard for family meals. The wholesome food she made was always from scratch. We always knew what time dinner was served, and when we came in after playing outside, the aroma answered the obvious question. Fresh vegetables surrounded mouthwatering main dishes. It's no wonder we spent quality time together as a family around the dinner table day after day.

I want my children to experience this kitchen conviviality, and I'm sure you do, too. But my life, like most of yours, is distinctly different from my mom's. In addition to working inside my home, I work outside of it, too. After work, school activities often have us on the road, heading to and from practices and meetings. Even in the face of a busy lifestyle, I refuse to give up the family dinner tradition. Like you, I recognize that wholesome meals fuel our families' bodies, and that the quality time we spend together is priceless.

If you share these same ideals, ***Southern Living*** *Busy Moms' Weeknight Favorites* was created just for you. It's filled with 130 fast recipes with serious kid appeal for the simplest of palates to the more discriminating palates of parents. Simple menus with quick-to-fix sides help you to quickly round out meals. Grocery lists take the guesswork out of shopping. There's even a nutritional analysis for each recipe as requested by so many moms.

"I want my children to experience this kitchen conviviality, and I'm sure you do, too."

Our hope is that the recipes in this book give you just what you need to prepare wholesome meals in record time. After all, as moms we all want to spend more time enjoying our family suppers than preparing them.

Elizabeth Taliaferro
Editor

special thanks

An exceptional group of moms joined us in our workplace and spent hours answering questions about the cooking challenges they face as Busy Moms. These women gladly rolled up their sleeves and joined our Test Kitchens staff to test dozens of recipes featured in this book.

In addition, we want to thank the many other real–life moms for their willingness to try new recipes in their homes and share their personal comments and tips.

All of these experiences fill this book with resourceful ideas and our staff with a whole new group of friendships.

Clockwise starting at top left:
Carrie Dickie, San Clemente, CA;
Betsey Bishop, Warrenton, VA;
Michelle Smith-Rapoza,
East Greenwich, RI;
Shannon Warner, McKinney, TX;
Chris Borisch, Oregon City, OR;
Elsa-Maria Lorenzo, Glenn Allen, VA;
Doran Helton, Hoover, AL;
Kimberly D'Alelio, Boxford, MA;
Angie Knapp, Chatham, IL;
Suzanne Opersteny,
Universal City, TX

5 Super Solutions *for weeknight bliss*

1 GET ORGANIZED. Store commonly used ingredients and tools in the same place every time. Make it a habit and you'll quickly see how efficiency can save you time and teach your kids the value of staying organized.

• Alphabetize spices and seasonings so they're quick to find. If you have room, dried seasonings store best in the freezer. If you store them in a cabinet, place them in a cool area away from heat or light.

• Store wooden spoons, rubber and metal spatulas, tongs, wire whisks, cooking spoons and forks, potato masher, kitchen shears, basting brush, and a ladle in large decorative crocks or jars near your cooktop and mixing center. Store potholders close to the oven, cooktop, and microwave for quick access.

• Stock your pantry, refrigerator, and freezer with commonly used food items.

• For easy access, stock a drawer or rack inside a cabinet door near your work area with aluminum foil, plastic wrap, wax paper, several sizes of food storage bags, and parchment paper.

• Attach a magnetic shopping list to the refrigerator door for jotting down items to purchase as you think of them. Train the kids to list any needs they have like school supplies or toiletries on the same list.

• Buy heavy items in bulk or in large quantities several times a year. Having laundry products, dishwashing detergent, cleaning products, bottled water, sports drinks, or soft drinks on hand speeds weekly shopping trips, lightens the grocery load, and prevents frustration of running out at a crucial time.

2 MAKE MEAL PLANS.

Prepare and grocery shop for supper meals before the chaos of the week sets in. Set aside some uninterrupted time—about 15 minutes—to plan a week's worth of meals and your shopping list. The process will take less time, once you have a routine in place.

• Develop a repertoire of about 12 recipes your family loves. Bookmark them with sticky notes or keep copies in a binder.

• Check your family calendar to determine just how many nights you'll be able to cook.

• Decide on one main dish per weeknight meal along with simple sides, then prepare your grocery list. Vary the side dishes to introduce the kids to new foods and to prevent boredom.

• Do the bulk of your shopping once a week at a full-service supermarket; then plan one or two return trips to pick up perishables. Lots of moms make those return trips to farmers markets or splurge with visits to specialty grocers where access in and out is faster than large chain grocery stores.

• Create a blank shopping list on your computer in categories that match the aisles in the grocery store. Categories might include: canned goods/convenience items; pasta/rice/grains; cleaning supplies/toiletries; deli/bakery foods; produce; meats; dairy; and frozen foods. Print several lists at a time to keep handy.

• Try to shop before noon, any day of the week—it's typically the least busy shopping time of the day.

• Avoid shopping when you or the kids are hungry to prevent making unhealthy impulse

purchases. And choose a checkout line without a candy display.

• Put your groceries through checkout in categories. Once you arrive home, you'll be able to put away items quickly because they'll already be sorted.

• If you're shopping with little ones, take advantage of customer service, and request assistance to your car. While you secure seat belts, a grocery store employee can load the groceries.

• As soon as you arrive home, record the date of purchase with a permanent marker on boxes and packages to easily identify the ones that need to be used first.

3 COOK QUICKLY.

COOK QUICKLY. Work faster not harder by taking advantage of grocery and kitchen resources.

• Read through recipes or package instructions and gather ingredients and equipment before you begin.

• Avoid preparing too much food for one meal. Select two menu items, three at the most, for each weeknight meal.

• Purchase presliced, prechopped, and prewashed produce. Sometimes it's slightly more expensive, but the trade-off is in the time saved from prepping and cleaning. Always check the freshness date, and look closely at the cut edges of the produce for signs of aging.

• Use kitchen shears to chop canned tomatoes right in the open can and to snip lettuces for quick salads. Kitchen shears are also great to get into cantankerous packaged goods. Chop small amounts of ingredients quickly with a handheld food chopper or mini food processor.

• Spend a little more on quality disposable products. Most moms agree it pays off when they need to perform without fail.

• Put disposable products to good use. Measure ingredients on paper plates, wax paper, pop-up foil sheets, or paper towels. Line baking pans or broiler pans with aluminum foil before cooking. Use disposable cutting sheets for meats, poultry, and fish to eliminate the need to sanitize cutting boards and reduce the risk of cross-contamination.

• Begin with meats purchased in their closest-to-usable form, such as chicken tenderloins, fish fillets, or peeled and deveined shrimp.

• Pack single servings of leftovers in individual microwave-safe containers. Or use zip-top freezer bags, which are sturdy enough to stack easily and don't take up much space.

• Cook basic foods in bulk. For instance, brown ground beef with chopped onion, and freeze it in zip-top freezer bags. When you need a quick meal, thaw a portion for tacos, sloppy joes, or spaghetti.

• Round out meals with convenience food products. There's rarely time to prepare every part of a weeknight meal so purchase side dishes that are ready-made, such as the popular examples that follow.

Popular Foods Kits and Conveniences

Frozen vegetables are prepped and ready to cook or steam in the microwave. Look for brands that give instructions for microwaving directly in the bag or box, which leaves no dishes to clean up.

Microwaveable mashed potatoes in a variety of flavors such as garlic, sour cream and chives, and country-style.

Microwaveable precooked rice like whole grain brown, Spanish, and roasted chicken flavor. The product is shelf stable and ready to serve in seconds.

Ready-made side dishes from your grocer's deli. Most deli departments will allow you to sample to determine what sides are to your liking.

Precut fruit and vegetables from the produce department or self-serve deli salad bars.

Salad kits such as Asian, Ranch, or Caesar typically come complete with dressings and toppings.

• Use your microwave oven. It's great for cooking vegetables, boiling water, toasting nuts, warming flour tortillas, cooking bacon, and melting butter.

• Use zip-top bags to make crumbs for toppings and to marinate meats, poultry, or vegetables.

• Empty the dishwasher before you begin cooking, or have the kids do it.

• Encourage family participation with simple, kid-friendly tasks. It's also a great way to begin teaching basic kitchen skills while saving Mom time. And there's an extra perk for parents of picky eaters: Kids are usually more willing to eat something they had a hand in cooking. See task suggestions based on age below.

Ages and Suggested Kitchen Tasks

Age 3: Wash fruits and vegetables, and stir ingredients in large deep bowls.

Age 4: Open packages, squeeze citrus, measure and spoon out cookies, and tear lettuce.

Age 5-6: Measure ingredients, set the table, and cut soft foods with a fork or table knife.

Age 7-8: Find ingredients in the refrigerator, pantry or spice rack, knead dough, and crack eggs.

Age 9-12: Open cans, use small appliances, empty the dishwasher, follow a recipe, and prepare meals with minimal ingredients.

Age 13-16: Prepare recipes with multiple ingredients.

4 COOK HEALTHY. Put these simple tips to work to improve nutrition and encourage smart eating habits.

• Select canned fruits in their own juice rather than syrup. Trim excess fat from poultry and meats before cooking.

• Use low-fat dairy products, salad dressings, mayonnaise, and other condiments.

• Avoid adding salt to recipes when possible. Experiment with salt-free seasoning blends or squeezing fresh lemon or lime juice over foods.

• Sneak in more nutrition in foods by using the suggestions below.

Healthy Additions
• Stir broccoli, chopped tomato, mushrooms, carrots, or raisins into plain rice or couscous.
• Use generous amounts of fruit in smoothies.
• Add chopped apple to tuna salad.
• Add cubed pineapple or cantaloupe to chicken kabobs.
• Add grated carrots, chopped zucchini, and diced tomatoes to spaghetti sauce.
• Cut carrots and zucchini into long diagonal slices and serve with salsa instead of chips.
• Put lettuce and tomato on your sandwiches.
• Eat a cluster of grapes instead of chips.

• Cook with low-fat methods such as broiling, oven-frying, grilling, and steaming.

• After cooking ground meat, drain it thoroughly in a colander and pat with paper towels to remove excess fat. If you're planning to return the meat to the pan, wipe it also with a paper towel.

• Reduce the fat in soups and gravies by chilling them first and skimming the fat off the top.

• Enjoy a healthy splurge. Satisfy a weeknight sweet tooth with frozen fruit juice pops, low-fat ice cream sandwiches, or fresh berries over frozen yogurt.

• Learn to control the kids' portion sizes according to hunger level, fullness, and by the example you set. Begin by serving appropriate serving sizes. Teach the family to eyeball serving sizes by comparing them to common objects popular to adults and youngsters.

Portion Size Comparisons

3 oz. meat, fish, and poultry	=	deck of playing cards
2 Tbsp. peanut butter	=	ping pong ball
1 cup serving	=	baseball or tennis ball
$1/2$ cup serving	=	small computer mouse
1 oz. Cheddar cheese	=	6 small dice
1 small piece fruit	=	lightbulb

5 PROMOTE A SENSE OF FAMILY.

Joining together for a meal has a greater purpose than simply eating. No matter what the size of your family, mealtime is for talking, sharing, listening, learning, and supporting one another.

• Start and end meals together to encourage a sense of family and to show respect.

• Establish a fun family tradition with a "spaghetti night" or another favorite dish on the same day each week. The tradition doesn't need to be elaborate to be successful—just dependable.

• Turn off the television to strengthen conversation and improve focus on the activity at hand—dinner. Consider playing easy listening music at a low volume.

• Keep dinner conversations light and upbeat. Mealtime is not the time for criticism or discipline. If the conversation moves in a tense direction, change the subject and address the matter later.

• Ask the kids some questions that require more than one-word answers to encourage conversation. Teach them how to initiate discussion as well.

• If your home or cell phone rings during dinner, let the answering machine take a message.

• After the meal, say "thank you" to those who prepared the meal, and offer to take dishes to the sink, help load the dishwasher, or put away food.

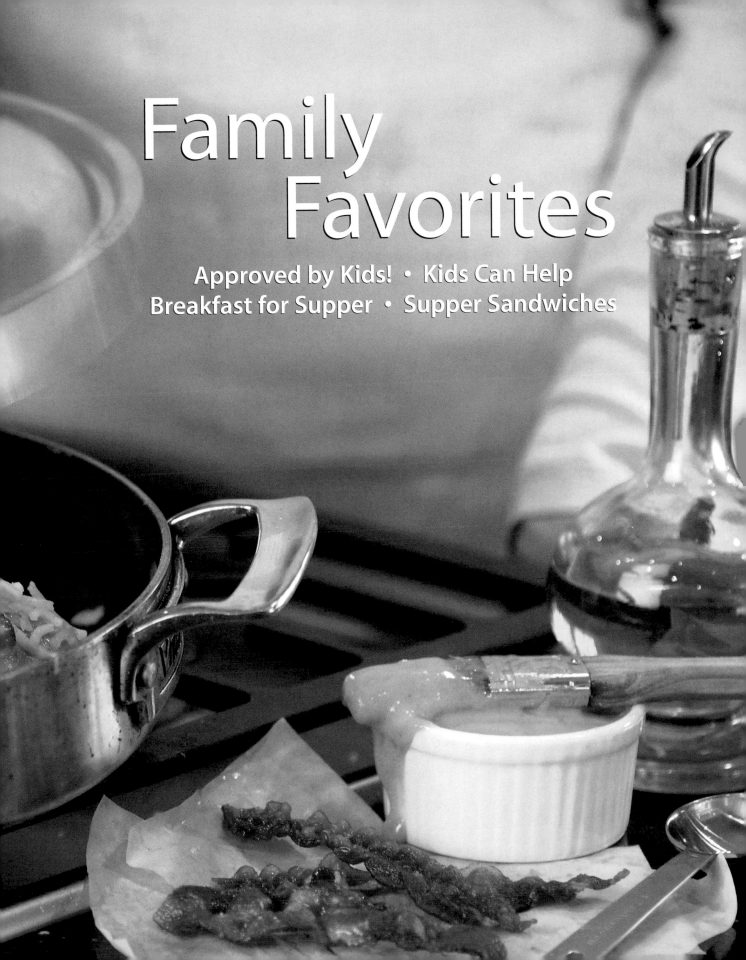

Family Favorites

Approved by Kids! • **Kids Can Help**
Breakfast for Supper • **Supper Sandwiches**

Prep: 10 min. ✷ **Cook:** 30 min.

Sloppy Joe Squares

Makes 6 servings

"This recipe is so easy. I still have enough energy to make it after late afternoon baseball games. With the cheesy filling and sloppy joe flavor, it's a winner. My home team cleans their plates!"
—Debra L., Madison, AL

MENU IDEA FOR 6

- Sloppy Joe Squares
- Iceberg lettuce wedges with cherry tomatoes

GROCERIES NEEDED

Check staples: dried onion flakes, milk, sesame seeds (optional), salad dressing

- 1 lb. lean ground beef
- 1 (8-oz.) can tomato sauce
- 1 (1.5-oz.) package sloppy joe mix
- 2 (8-oz.) cans refrigerated reduced-fat crescent rolls (we tested with Pillsbury)
- 1 cup (4 oz.) shredded Cheddar cheese
- 1 head iceberg lettuce
- 1 pt. cherry tomatoes

PER ENTRÉE SERVING:
CALORIES 525 (45% from fat); FAT 26g (sat 9.8g, mono 5.1g, poly 0.4g); PROTEIN 25.9g; CARB 40.1g; FIBER 0.3g; CHOL 69mg; IRON 2.1mg; SODIUM 1472mg; CALC 148mg

---

1 lb. lean ground beef
1 (8-oz.) can tomato sauce
1 cup water
1 (1.5-oz.) package sloppy joe mix
1 tsp. dried onion flakes

2 (8-oz.) cans refrigerated reduced-fat crescent rolls
1 cup (4 oz.) shredded Cheddar cheese
1 Tbsp. milk
1 Tbsp. sesame seeds (optional)

1. Preheat oven to 425°. Brown ground beef in a large skillet over medium-high heat, stirring until it crumbles and is no longer pink. Drain and pat dry with paper towels. Wipe skillet clean. Return beef to skillet; stir in tomato sauce and next 3 ingredients. Bring to a boil; reduce heat, and simmer 10 minutes, stirring occasionally.

2. Unroll 1 can crescent rolls into a lightly greased 13- x 9-inch baking dish. Press seams together to seal perforations. Spread beef mixture over dough; sprinkle with cheese. Unroll remaining can of rolls over cheese, pinching seams together to seal perforations. Brush dough with milk, and sprinkle with sesame seeds, if desired. Bake at 425° for 15 minutes or until golden.

Flavor Change: A package of taco seasoning mix works great in place of the sloppy joe mix.

MENU IDEA FOR 8

- Golden Macaroni and Cheese
- Tomato soup
- Purple seedless grapes

GROCERIES NEEDED

Check staples: all-purpose flour, onion salt, milk, butter, pepper

- 1 (8-oz.) package elbow macaroni
- 4$^1/_2$ cups (18 oz.) shredded sharp Cheddar cheese
- 4 sandwich bread slices
- 4 (18.3-oz.) containers Italian tomato soup with basil and garlic (such as Campbell's Select Gold Label)
- 2 lb. purple seedless grapes

PER ENTRÉE SERVING:
CALORIES 465 (56% from fat); FAT 28.8g (sat 18.4g, mono 2.1g, poly 0.8g); PROTEIN 20.1g; CARB 31.5g; FIBER 1.2g; CHOL 77mg; IRON 1.2mg; SODIUM 880mg; CALC 536mg

Prep: 10 min. ❊ **Cook:** 57 min.

Golden Macaroni and Cheese

Makes 8 servings

"Instead of using a whisk and mixing bowl in the second step, I combine the flour, onion salt, and milk in a quart jar with the lid screwed on tightly. Then I just shake the mixture until there are no lumps. The kids love to 'shake it up,' too." —Julie M., Alabaster, AL

1 (8-oz.) package elbow macaroni (about 2 cups uncooked macaroni)

$^1/_4$ cup all-purpose flour
1 tsp. onion salt
2 cups milk
4$^1/_2$ cups (18 oz.) shredded sharp Cheddar cheese, divided
1 cup soft breadcrumbs (4 sandwich bread slices, crusts removed)
$^1/_4$ cup butter or margarine, melted
Garnish: pepper

1. Preheat oven to 350°. Cook macaroni according to package directions; drain well.

2. Combine flour and onion salt in a large bowl; gradually whisk in milk until blended. Stir in 3$^1/_2$ cups cheese and macaroni. Pour mixture into a lightly greased 13- x 9-inch baking dish or 2 (11-inch) oval baking dishes. Sprinkle with breadcrumbs and remaining 1 cup cheese; drizzle with melted butter. Bake, uncovered, at 350° for 45 minutes or until golden. Garnish with pepper, if desired.

Prep Note: A small amount of soft breadcrumbs, which form a crisp, buttery topping, is simple to make in a mini-food processor. Tear ordinary sandwich bread into small pieces and pulse to form small crumbs.

Prep: 15 min. ☀ **Cook:** 1 hr., 10 min. ☀ **Other:** 10 min.

Cheeseburger Meat Loaf

Makes 4 servings

It does a mom's heart good to see her family enjoy a homestyle meal like this one—especially since it takes only 15 minutes to prep the meat loaf. The simple sides are microwaveable.

1 lb. lean ground beef
1 cup (4 oz.) shredded sharp Cheddar cheese
¾ cup uncooked regular oats
½ cup milk
2 Tbsp. minced onion
1 large egg
1 tsp. Worcestershire sauce
½ tsp. salt
½ tsp. dry mustard
¼ tsp. garlic powder
¼ tsp. pepper
1 cup chili sauce

1. Preheat oven to 350°. Combine first 11 ingredients in a large bowl; stir just until blended. Shape mixture into a loaf, and place in an ungreased 8- x 4-inch loafpan.

2. Bake at 350° for 30 minutes. Pour chili sauce over meat loaf, and bake 40 more minutes or until meat is no longer pink in center. Let stand for 10 minutes. Drain and cut into 8 slices.

Cleanup Tip: Before placing the shaped meat loaf in the loafpan, line the loafpan with aluminum foil.

MENU IDEA FOR 4

- No-Bake Cheesy Ziti Toss
- Caesar salad
- Italian bread

GROCERIES NEEDED

Check staples: pepper

- 1 (16-oz.) package ziti (we tested with Barilla)
- 1 (15-oz.) can pasta-style tomatoes
- 1¹/₂ cups (6 oz.) shredded Cheddar-mozzarella cheese blend
- 1 small red bell pepper
- 1 small jar oil-packed dried tomatoes
- 1 small jar kalamata olives or 1 (4¹/₂-oz.) can chopped ripe olives
- 1 bunch fresh basil
- 1 (10-oz.) package Caesar salad kit (such as Dole)
- 1 loaf Italian bread

PER ENTRÉE SERVING:
CALORIES 461 (33% from fat); FAT 16.8g (sat 7.4g, mono 2.3g, poly 0.4g); PROTEIN 19g; CARB 59.8g; FIBER 7.6g; CHOL 30mg; IRON 2.6mg; SODIUM 1254mg; CALC 264mg

Prep: 15 min. ❋ **Cook:** 16 min.

No-Bake Cheesy Ziti Toss

Makes 4 servings

This meatless main dish provides ample protein for your growing family thanks to the Cheddar cheese and the generous serving size.

½ (16-oz.) package ziti

1 (15-oz.) can pasta-style tomatoes, undrained

1½ cups (6 oz.) shredded Cheddar-mozzarella cheese blend

1 small red bell pepper, chopped

½ cup oil-packed dried tomatoes, drained and chopped

⅓ cup chopped kalamata or pitted ripe olives

⅓ cup chopped fresh basil

½ tsp. black pepper

1. Cook ziti according to package directions; drain well.

2. Meanwhile, stir together tomatoes and remaining 6 ingredients in a large serving bowl. Add hot pasta, and toss gently.

Substitution Note: If fresh basil isn't available, use a can of pasta-style tomatoes with Italian herbs.

MENU IDEA FOR 8

- Three-Cheese Pasta Bake
- Tossed salad
- Italian bread

GROCERIES NEEDED

Check staples: large eggs, grated Parmesan cheese, salad dressing

- 1 (16-oz.) package ziti
- 2 (10-oz.) containers light refrigerated Alfredo sauce (we tested with Buitoni)
- 1 (8-oz.) container reduced-fat sour cream
- 1 (15-oz.) container part-skim ricotta cheese
- 1 bunch fresh parsley
- 1½ cups (6 oz.) shredded part-skim mozzarella cheese
- 1 (16-oz.) package crisp lettuce
- 2 tomatoes
- 1 loaf Italian bread

PER ENTRÉE SERVING:
CALORIES 475 (33% from fat); FAT 17.6g (sat 11.2g, mono 1.7g, poly 0.3g); PROTEIN 26.2g; CARB 55.2g; FIBER 1.9g; CHOL 121mg; IRON 2.2mg; SODIUM 979mg; CALC 423mg

---

Prep: 20 min. ❄ **Cook:** 30 min.

Three-Cheese Pasta Bake

Makes 8 servings

"Having three quiet boys at the dinner table is a guarantee that they thought this recipe was delicious. My 8-year-old said, 'It tastes like a roller coaster of flavor that keeps on going higher.' "—Jodi W., Maple Valley, WA

1 (16-oz.) package ziti

2 (10-oz.) containers light refrigerated Alfredo sauce
1 (8-oz.) container reduced-fat sour cream

1 (15-oz.) container part-skim ricotta cheese
2 large eggs, lightly beaten
¼ cup grated Parmesan cheese
¼ cup chopped fresh parsley
1½ cups (6 oz.) shredded part-skim mozzarella cheese

1. Preheat oven to 350°. Cook ziti according to package directions; drain well.

2. Stir together Alfredo sauce and sour cream in a large bowl; add ziti, stirring until blended. Spoon half of mixture into a lightly greased 13- x 9-inch baking dish.

3. Stir together ricotta cheese and next 3 ingredients; spread evenly over pasta mixture in dish. Spoon remaining pasta mixture evenly over ricotta cheese layer; sprinkle with mozzarella cheese. Bake, uncovered, at 350° for 30 minutes or until bubbly.

Health Note: This traditionally high-calorie recipe is a cross between fettuccine Alfredo and baked macaroni and cheese. Using lightened versions of four ingredients saves 137 calories per serving when compared to the traditional recipe. Best of all, your family will never know the difference.

Prep: 5 min. ❋ **Cook:** 18 min.

Honey Mustard-and-Bacon Smothered Chicken

Makes 4 servings

Our original recipe had twice as much butter, oil, and cheese, but we retested and realized less was plenty to get the job done.

MENU IDEA FOR 4

- Honey Mustard-and-Bacon Smothered Chicken
- Steamed green beans
- Apple wedges

GROCERIES NEEDED

Check staples: salt, pepper, butter, vegetable oil

- 4 (6-oz.) skinned and boned chicken breasts
- 1 small jar honey-mustard dressing
- 8 fully cooked bacon slices (we tested with Ready Crisp)
- ¼ cup (1 oz.) shredded Mexican four-cheese blend
- 1 lb. fresh or frozen green beans
- 2 apples

PER ENTRÉE SERVING:
CALORIES 372 (46% from fat); FAT 19g (sat 6.3g, mono 2.8g, poly 2.1g); PROTEIN 44.2g; CARB 3.3g; FIBER 0g; CHOL 122mg; IRON 1.3mg; SODIUM 578mg; CALC 70mg

4 (6-oz.) skinned and boned chicken breasts
¼ tsp. salt
¼ tsp. pepper

1 Tbsp. butter or margarine
1 Tbsp. vegetable oil
¼ cup honey-mustard dressing
8 fully cooked bacon slices
¼ cup (1 oz.) shredded Mexican four-cheese blend

1. Sprinkle chicken with salt and pepper.

2. Melt butter with oil in a large skillet over medium-high heat; add chicken, and cook 8 minutes on each side or until done. Reduce heat to medium-low; brush chicken with honey-mustard dressing. Top each chicken breast with 2 bacon slices, and sprinkle with cheese. Cover and cook 2 minutes or until cheese melts.

Shopping Note: Fully cooked bacon slices eliminate the hassle of cooking and cleanup. Purchase several packages when they're on sale, and freeze them up to 3 months to have on hand.

Crunchy Catfish
Fingers

MENU IDEA FOR 8

- Crunchy Catfish Fingers
- Creamy coleslaw
- Deli baked beans

GROCERIES NEEDED

Check staples: seasoned salt, fat-free milk, Dijon mustard, cornstarch, pepper, vegetable cooking spray

- 8 (4-oz.) catfish fillets
- 1 box crispy corn cereal squares (we tested with Corn Chex)
- 1 jar tartar sauce or 1 bottle ketchup (optional)
- 2 (16-oz.) packages coleslaw mix
- 1 bottle coleslaw dressing
- 2 pt. deli baked beans

PER ENTRÉE SERVING:
CALORIES 335 (32% from fat); FAT 11.8g (sat 2.8g, mono 5.5g, poly 2.5g); PROTEIN 27g; CARB 28.9g; FIBER 0.6g; CHOL 72mg; IRON 8.4mg; SODIUM 568mg; CALC 159mg

Prep: 20 min. ❋ **Cook:** 22 min.

Crunchy Catfish Fingers

Makes 8 servings

Lightly coating the fish with cooking spray before baking assures a light, crisp coating. For dipping, some kids like tartar sauce while others love ketchup.

8	(4-oz.) catfish fillets
¾	tsp. seasoned salt, divided
1½	cups fat-free milk
2	Tbsp. Dijon mustard
5	cups crispy corn cereal squares, crushed
¼	cup cornstarch
½	tsp. pepper
	Vegetable cooking spray

Tartar sauce or ketchup (optional)

1. Preheat oven to 375°. Cut each fillet lengthwise into 3 strips. Sprinkle fish evenly with ½ tsp. seasoned salt.

2. Whisk together milk and mustard in a small bowl. Combine crushed cereal, cornstarch, pepper, and remaining ¼ tsp. seasoned salt in a shallow bowl. Dip fish in milk mixture; dredge in cereal mixture. Arrange fish fingers on a baking sheet coated with cooking spray. Lightly coat fish with cooking spray.

3. Bake at 375° for 20 to 22 minutes or until fish flakes with a fork. Serve with tartar sauce or ketchup, if desired.

Prep: 7 min. ☀ **Cook:** 37 min.

Upside-Down Pizza Casserole

Makes 8 servings

"Pizza! That's the magic word that makes this recipe a hit at my house. I love it because it's very easy and not intimidating." —Shannon W., McKinney, TX

2 (16-oz.) packages ground pork sausage
2 medium onions, chopped
1 small green bell pepper, chopped
3 tsp. dried basil, divided
1 tsp. fennel seeds (optional)
¼ cup all-purpose flour
1 (26-oz.) jar tomato-and-basil pasta sauce
2 cups (8 oz.) shredded mozzarella cheese, divided

1 (13.8-oz.) can refrigerated pizza crust dough
1 Tbsp. olive oil
2 Tbsp. grated Parmesan cheese

1. Preheat oven to 425°. Cook sausage, onions, bell pepper, 2 tsp. basil, and fennel seeds, if desired, in a large skillet over medium-high heat about 10 minutes, stirring until sausage crumbles, is no longer pink, and onions are tender. Drain well. Return mixture to pan, and add flour; stir until blended. Stir in pasta sauce. Bring to a boil over medium-high heat, stirring constantly. Spoon mixture into a lightly greased 13- x 9-inch baking dish. Sprinkle with 1½ cups mozzarella cheese.

2. Unroll pizza crust dough, and place on cheese and sausage mixture. Tuck edges of crust into baking dish, if necessary. Brush with olive oil, and sprinkle with remaining ½ cup mozzarella cheese, Parmesan cheese, and remaining 1 tsp. basil. Bake at 425° for 20 minutes or until golden.

Chicken Spaghetti Bake

Makes 6 servings

"We loved how cheesy this recipe turned out. For me, I like how quickly it came together the very first time I made it. Now that I'm familiar with it, it'll be a cinch to assemble."—Bianca G., Hoover, AL

MENU IDEA FOR 6

- Chicken Spaghetti Bake
- Green beans
- Garlic bread

GROCERIES NEEDED

Check staples: vegetable oil, Worcestershire sauce, salad dressing

- 1 (8-oz.) package spaghetti
- 1 medium onion
- 1 small red bell pepper
- 2 (14.5-oz.) cans diced tomatoes with basil, garlic, and oregano
- 1 (5-oz.) jar processed cheese spread (we tested with Old English)
- 3 cups chopped cooked chicken or 1 deli rotisserie chicken
- 1¹/₂ cups (6 oz.) shredded sharp Cheddar cheese
- 1¹/₂ lb. fresh or frozen green beans
- 1 loaf garlic bread

PER ENTRÉE SERVING:
CALORIES 509 (36% from fat); FAT 20.4g (sat 10.8g, mono 1.9g, poly 1.8g); PROTEIN 38.3g; CARB 42.8g; FIBER 3.2g; CHOL 103mg; IRON 4.2mg; SODIUM 1537mg; CALC 311mg

1 (8-oz.) package spaghetti

1 Tbsp. vegetable oil
1 medium onion, chopped
¹/₂ cup chopped red bell pepper
2 (14.5-oz.) cans diced tomatoes with basil, garlic, and oregano, undrained
2 tsp. Worcestershire sauce

1 (5-oz.) jar processed cheese spread

3 cups chopped cooked chicken
1¹/₂ cups (6 oz.) shredded sharp Cheddar cheese

1. Preheat oven to 350°. Cook pasta according to package directions. Drain well.

2. Heat oil in a large nonstick skillet over medium-high heat. Add onion and pepper; sauté until tender. Add tomatoes and Worcestershire sauce; bring to a boil. Reduce heat, and simmer, uncovered, 8 to 10 minutes.

3. Remove metal lid from cheese spread jar; microwave at HIGH 30 to 45 seconds or until melted, stirring once. Add to tomato mixture, stirring well.

4. Combine pasta, tomato mixture, and chicken in a large bowl, stirring until blended. Spoon into a lightly greased 11- x 7-inch baking dish; sprinkle with Cheddar cheese. Bake, uncovered, at 350° for 15 minutes or until cheese melts.

Shopping Note: The chopped meat from a deli rotisserie chicken is just the right amount for this recipe.

Prep: 10 min. ❋ **Cook:** 15 min.

Pork Loin Chops with Cinnamon Apples

Makes 4 servings

"The sage in this recipe adds great taste without being overpowering to the kids. They really gobble it up when I slice the apples so thinly that every bite of pork gets a bite of apple, too." —Danielle N., Las Vegas, NV

MENU IDEA FOR 4

- Pork Loin Chops with Cinnamon Apples
- Buttered poppy seed noodles
- Green peas

GROCERIES NEEDED

Check staples: dried rubbed sage, salt, pepper, vegetable oil, vegetable cooking spray, butter, brown sugar, ground cinnamon

- 4 (4-oz.) boneless pork chops (about ¹/₂ inch thick)
- 4 medium Granny Smith or Braeburn apples
- 1 (7.5-oz.) bottle frozen lemon juice (we tested with Minute Maid)
- 8 oz. wide egg noodles
- 1 small jar poppy seeds
- 1 bunch fresh parsley
- 1 (16-oz.) package frozen green peas

PER ENTRÉE SERVING:
CALORIES 287 (43% from fat);
FAT 13.7g (sat 5.2g, mono 5.8g,
poly 1.4g); PROTEIN 24.1g;
CARB 16.8g; FIBER 1.7g;
CHOL 76mg; IRON 1.2mg;
SODIUM 385mg; CALC 37mg

1   tsp. dried rubbed sage
¹/₂ tsp. salt
¹/₄ tsp. pepper
4   (4-oz.) boneless pork chops (about ¹/₂ inch thick)

¹/₂ tsp. vegetable oil
Vegetable cooking spray

1   tsp. butter or margarine
4   small Granny Smith apples, peeled and sliced
1   Tbsp. brown sugar
1   tsp. lemon juice
¹/₂ tsp. ground cinnamon
Dash of salt

1. Combine first 3 ingredients, and sprinkle over pork.

2. Heat oil in a large nonstick skillet coated with cooking spray over medium heat. Add pork; cook 3 minutes on each side or until done. Remove pork from skillet. Cover and keep warm.

3. Melt butter in skillet over medium heat. Add apples and remaining ingredients, and cook 5 minutes or until tender, stirring often. Serve apples with pork.

Shopping Note: Braeburn apples substitute nicely for the Granny Smith apples. Consider using apples that have already been peeled, cored, and sliced for convenience. You'll need about 4 cups.

Side Dish Note: Cook egg noodles according to package directions. Drain and return to pan. Add 1 Tbsp. butter, ¹/₂ tsp. poppy seeds, and 2 Tbsp. minced parsley; toss until butter melts.

Prep: 15 min. ✳ Cook: 23 min.

Chicken Pot Pies

Makes 4 servings

This recipe and those that follow have easy preparation techniques that children will enjoy helping with. In this case, the kids can use a small cereal bowl as a guide for cutting the dough into circles. The crusts cook separately on a baking sheet and are then placed over the filling, so you won't need to use ovenproof bowls.

½ (15-oz.) package refrigerated
  piecrusts
Vegetable cooking spray

2 Tbsp. all-purpose flour
1 tsp. dried rubbed sage
½ tsp. salt
½ tsp. pepper
1 lb. chicken breast tenders, cut into
  bite-sized pieces

1¼ cups water
1½ cups frozen mixed vegetables
1 cup fresh mushrooms, quartered
1 (10¾-oz.) can reduced-fat, reduced-
  sodium cream of chicken soup

1. Preheat oven to 425°. Cut 4 (4-inch) circles out of dough; discard remaining dough. Place dough circles on a baking sheet coated with cooking spray. Lightly coat dough with cooking spray; pierce top of dough circles with a fork. Bake at 425° for 8 minutes or until golden.

2. Combine flour, sage, salt, and pepper in a zip-top freezer bag; add chicken. Seal bag, and toss to coat.

3. Heat a large nonstick skillet coated with cooking spray over medium-high heat. Add chicken mixture; cook 5 minutes, browning on all sides. Stir in water, scraping pan to loosen browned bits. Stir in vegetables, mushrooms, and soup; bring to a boil. Reduce heat, and cook 10 minutes. Spoon 1 cup chicken mixture into each of 4 (1-cup) ramekins or bowls; top each serving with 1 crust circle.

MENU IDEA FOR 4

- Chicken Pot Pies
- Spinach-orange salad
- Vanilla ice cream

GROCERIES NEEDED

Check staples:
vegetable cooking spray, all-purpose flour, dried rubbed sage, salt, pepper

- 1 (15-oz.) package refrigerated piecrusts (we tested with Pillsbury)
- 1 lb. chicken breast tenders
- 1½ cups frozen mixed vegetables
- 1 cup fresh mushrooms
- 1 (10¾-oz.) can reduced-fat, reduced-sodium cream of chicken soup
- 1 (9-oz.) package fresh spinach (such as Fresh Express)
- 1 (11-oz.) can mandarin oranges
- 1 bottle poppy seed dressing
- ½ gal. vanilla ice cream

PER ENTRÉE SERVING:
CALORIES 440 (29% from fat);
FAT 14.2g (sat 5g, mono 0.4g, poly 0.4g); PROTEIN 31.8g;
CARB 44.6g; FIBER 3.6g;
CHOL 77mg; IRON 2mg;
SODIUM 869mg; CALC 40mg

MENU IDEA FOR 6

MENU IDEA FOR 6

- Chicken Burritos
- Yellow rice
- Black beans

GROCERIES NEEDED

Check staples: vegetable oil

- 1 medium onion
- 3 cups chopped cooked chicken or 1 deli rotisserie chicken
- 1 (10-oz.) can diced tomatoes with green chiles
- 1 (16-oz.) container refrigerated mild white cheese dip
- 6 (10-inch) flour tortillas
- 1½ cups (6 oz.) shredded Cheddar cheese (optional)
- 1 (8-oz.) package shredded iceberg lettuce (optional)
- 1 small jar salsa (optional)
- 1 (10-oz.) package yellow rice (such as Vigo)
- 2 (15-oz.) cans black beans

PER ENTRÉE SERVING:
CALORIES 560 (42% from fat);
FAT 26.3g (sat 12.3g, mono 2.9g,
poly 2.6g); PROTEIN 38.3g;
CARB 37.1g; FIBER 6.7g;
CHOL 97mg; IRON 0.9mg;
SODIUM 1391mg; CALC 275mg

Prep: 28 min. ❋ **Cook:** 31 min.

Chicken Burritos

Makes 6 servings

Let the kids fill the tortilla and roll them up.
While the burritos bake, set the table.

2 Tbsp. vegetable oil
1 medium onion, chopped
3 cups chopped cooked chicken
1 (10-oz.) can diced tomatoes with green chiles, drained well
1 (16-oz.) container refrigerated mild white cheese dip

6 (10-inch) flour tortillas

Toppings: shredded Cheddar cheese, shredded iceberg lettuce, salsa (optional)

1. Preheat oven to 350°. Heat oil in a large skillet over medium-high heat. Add onion; cook 5 minutes or until onion is tender. Add chicken and tomatoes; stir well. Microwave cheese dip according to package directions. Stir in just enough cheese dip to lightly coat the chicken.

2. Spoon about ¾ cup chicken mixture down center of each tortilla; roll up. Place burritos, seam side down, in a lightly greased 15- x 10-inch baking dish. Drizzle with remaining cheese dip.

3. Bake, covered, at 350° for 15 minutes. Uncover and bake 10 more minutes or until thoroughly heated. Serve with toppings, if desired.

Shopping Note: Look for white cheese dip in your grocer's dairy case, or pick up a pint from your local Mexican restaurant.

Prep: 10 min. ❋ **Cook:** 15 min.

Shepherd's Pie

Makes 8 servings

"My sons are all adults now living on their own. The youngest stops by regularly in search for food. The last time he did, this recipe had just come out of the oven. He wants the recipe! Thanks to the prepared mashed potatoes and precooked beef tips, kids of all ages can make this."—Carol B., Blue Springs, MO

MENU IDEA FOR 8
- Shepherd's Pie
- Lime sherbet

GROCERIES NEEDED

Check staples: butter, garlic powder

- 2 (17-oz.) packages fully cooked beef tips with gravy (we tested with Hormel)
- 1 (10-oz.) package frozen whole kernel corn
- 1 (10-oz.) package frozen sweet peas
- 1 (24-oz.) package refrigerated mashed potatoes (we tested with Country Crock)
- 1 (8-oz.) package cream cheese
- 1 cup (4 oz.) shredded sharp Cheddar cheese
- ½ gal. lime sherbet

PER ENTRÉE SERVING:
CALORIES 346 (47% from fat); FAT 17.9g (sat 9.2g, mono 1.8g, poly 0.3g); PROTEIN 23.8g; CARB 23.9g; FIBER 3.4g; CHOL 79mg; IRON 2.3mg; SODIUM 1045mg; CALC 163mg

2 (17-oz.) packages fully cooked beef tips with gravy
1 cup frozen whole kernel corn, thawed
1 cup frozen sweet peas, thawed

1 (24-oz.) package refrigerated mashed potatoes
½ (8-oz.) package cream cheese, softened
1 Tbsp. butter or margarine, softened
1 tsp. garlic powder
1 cup (4 oz.) shredded sharp Cheddar cheese

1. Preheat oven to 350°. Cook beef according to package directions. Spoon beef into a lightly greased 11- x 7-inch baking dish. Top with corn and peas; set aside.

2. Cook potatoes according to package directions; spoon potatoes into a bowl. Add cream cheese, butter, and garlic powder; beat at medium speed with an electric mixer until smooth. Spread potato mixture over vegetables; sprinkle with cheese.

3. Bake, uncovered, at 350° for 15 minutes or until thoroughly heated.

Get the Family Involved: Some youngsters are turned on to cooking if they can use an electric appliance like a mixer. For safety's sake, teach children how to use it properly, and never leave them to use it unattended.

Prep: 8 min. ✳ Cook: 40 min.

Tuna Noodle Casserole

Makes 4 servings

"My mom made a dish very similar to this one when I was a child. So when we have this recipe, it reminds me to tell my kids details about my childhood as we enjoy supper." —Allison P., Cumming, GA

MENU IDEA FOR 4

- Tuna Casserole
- Apple wedges

GROCERIES NEEDED

Check staples: pepper

- 1 (16-oz.) package uncooked wide egg noodles
- 1¼ cups (5 oz.) shredded Cheddar cheese
- 1 (10¾-oz.) can cream of mushroom soup
- 1 (8.5-oz.) can sweet peas
- 1 (6-oz.) can solid white tuna in spring water
- 1 (5-oz.) can evaporated milk
- 1 small onion
- 1 box tiny fish-shaped crackers (we tested with Pepperidge Farm)
- 2 apples

PER ENTRÉE SERVING:
CALORIES 480 (46% from fat); FAT 24.4g (sat 12.1g, mono 6.5g, poly 2.5g); PROTEIN 25g; CARB 39.3g; FIBER 2.5g; CHOL 83mg; IRON 3.5mg; SODIUM 1434mg; CALC 397mg

---

3 cups uncooked wide egg noodles
1¼ cups (5 oz.) shredded Cheddar cheese, divided
1 (10¾-oz.) can cream of mushroom soup
1 (8.5-oz.) can sweet peas, drained
1 (6-oz.) can solid white tuna in spring water, drained and flaked
1 (5-oz.) can evaporated milk
⅓ cup finely chopped onion
½ tsp. pepper

1 cup tiny fish-shaped crackers

1. Preheat oven to 350°. Cook noodles according to package directions; drain. Stir together cooked noodles, 1 cup cheese, soup, and next 5 ingredients in a bowl; pour into a lightly greased 1½-qt. baking dish.

2. Bake, covered, at 350° for 30 minutes. Uncover and sprinkle with remaining cheese and crackers. Bake 5 more minutes or until thoroughly heated.

Get the Family Involved: Involve even the smallest children when making this recipe. Place the ingredients in a large bowl and instruct them to stir gently so the chunks of tuna will hold their shape. Let them sprinkle the cheese and crunchy fish-shaped crackers over the top at the end.

MENU IDEA FOR 6

- Quick Quesadillas
- Guacamole salad

GROCERIES NEEDED

Check staples:
vegetable cooking spray

- 12 (6-inch) flour tortillas
- 1½ cups (6 oz.) shredded Monterey Jack cheese
- 1½ cups (6 oz.) shredded Cheddar cheese
- 2 (4-oz.) cans chopped green chiles
- 3 medium plum tomatoes
- 1 small jar salsa
- 1 (8-oz.) package shredded iceberg lettuce (such as Fresh Express Shreds)
- 1 pt. prepared guacamole

PER ENTRÉE SERVING:
CALORIES 421 (52% from fat);
FAT 24.1g (sat 11.4g, mono 5.2g, poly 0.7g); PROTEIN 21g;
CARB 31.5g; FIBER 1.5g;
CHOL 55mg; IRON 1.9mg;
SODIUM 1121mg; CALC 500mg

Prep: 10 min. ✳ **Cook:** 36 min.

Quick Quesadillas

Makes 6 servings

Cook all of these at the same time on a large nonstick pancake griddle, and cut the cooking time of this recipe to only 6 minutes.

12 (6-inch) flour tortillas
  Vegetable cooking spray
1½ cups (6 oz.) shredded Monterey Jack cheese
1½ cups (6 oz.) shredded Cheddar cheese
2 (4-oz.) cans chopped green chiles, undrained
3 medium plum tomatoes, chopped

¾ cup salsa

1. Place 1 flour tortilla in a small nonstick skillet coated with cooking spray. Sprinkle with ¼ cup of each shredded cheese, 1 Tbsp. chiles, and 3 Tbsp. tomatoes. Top with 1 tortilla, and coat with cooking spray. Cook quesadilla over low heat 2 to 3 minutes on each side or until golden. Remove from skillet; set aside.

2. Repeat procedure with remaining tortillas, cooking spray, cheeses, chiles, and tomatoes. Cut each quesadilla into 6 triangles. Serve with salsa.

Get the Family Involved: Let the little kids stand with you at the cooktop and sprinkle on the fillings. Children over 12 may be able to prepare this on their own.

44

Prep: 15 min. ✳ **Cook:** 20 min.

Pigs in a Blanket

Makes 8 servings

"I've found that it's worth it to purchase brand name crescent rolls.
They're easier to handle than some store brands."
—Shari H., Birmingham, AL

MENU IDEA FOR 8

- Pigs in a Blanket
- Strawberry smoothie

GROCERIES NEEDED

Check staples: coarse-grained mustard, light mayonnaise

- 16 oz. uncooked small link breakfast sausage
- 2 (8-oz.) cans refrigerated reduced-fat crescent rolls (we tested with Pillsbury)
- 1 small jar honey
- 2 pt. fresh or frozen strawberries
- 1 (32-oz.) container vanilla low-fat yogurt

PER 2 PIGS IN A BLANKET AND ABOUT 2 TBSP DIPPING SAUCE: CALORIES 416 (58% from fat); FAT 26.7g (sat 7.5g, mono 6.7g, poly 2.1g); PROTEIN 12.6g; CARB 29.2g; FIBER 0g; CHOL 43mg; IRON 0.7mg; SODIUM 1082mg; CALC 5mg

16 oz. uncooked small link breakfast sausage

2 (8-oz.) cans refrigerated reduced-fat crescent rolls

½ cup coarse-grained mustard
¼ cup light mayonnaise
2 Tbsp. honey

1. Preheat oven to 350°. Cook sausage according to package directions. Drain on paper towels.

2. Divide crescent rolls into individual triangles. Place 1 cooked sausage link in center of each dough triangle. Roll up, starting at wide end. Arrange on an ungreased baking sheet.

3. Bake at 350° for 10 to 15 minutes or until golden. While sausage rolls bake, stir together mustard, mayonnaise, and honey. Serve dipping sauce with sausage rolls.

Get the Family Involved: This classic recipe makes little mess and is ideal for kids to assemble. Even lopsided rolls shaped by little hands bake up just fine.

MENU IDEA FOR 5

- Barbecue Muffins
- Angel hair slaw
- Watermelon wedges

GROCERIES NEEDED

Check staples:
ketchup, brown sugar, apple cider vinegar, chili powder

- 1 (12-oz.) can refrigerated buttermilk biscuits
- ¹/₂ lb. lean ground beef
- ¹/₂ cup (2 oz.) shredded Cheddar cheese
- 1 (10-oz.) package angel hair coleslaw
- 1 bottle coleslaw dressing
- 1 small watermelon

PER 2 MUFFINS: CALORIES 311 (28% from fat); FAT 9.8g (sat 4.5g, mono 3.7g, poly 0.6g); PROTEIN 17.4g; CARB 38.1g; FIBER 0g; CHOL 41mg; IRON 2.9mg; SODIUM 821mg; CALC 91mg

Prep: 10 min. ✳ **Cook:** 20 min.

Barbecue Muffins

Makes 10 muffins

"All three of my kids loved this. And why not? With melted cheese, biscuits, and tangy beef—it's comfort food for children."—Antonia E., San Carlos, CA

1 (12-oz.) can refrigerated buttermilk biscuits

¹/₂ lb. lean ground beef
¹/₄ cup ketchup
1¹/₂ Tbsp. brown sugar
1¹/₂ tsp. apple cider vinegar
¹/₄ tsp. chili powder

¹/₂ cup (2 oz.) shredded Cheddar cheese

1. Preheat oven to 375°. Separate biscuits; pat or roll into 5-inch circles on a lightly floured surface, and press into lightly greased muffin pans.

2. Brown ground beef in a large skillet, stirring until it crumbles and is no longer pink. Drain and pat dry with paper towels. Wipe skillet clean. Return beef to skillet; stir in ketchup and next 3 ingredients. Spoon into muffin cups.

3. Bake at 375° for 15 minutes. Sprinkle with cheese, and bake 5 more minutes or until cheese melts. Cool in pan on a wire rack 5 minutes.

Healthy Cooking: Wiping the skillet clean with a paper towel in Step 2 assures getting rid of all excess fat.

Get the Family Involved: Pressing the biscuit dough into the muffin pans is so simple. Show the kids how with one circle of dough, and let them do the rest while you cook the filling.

MENU IDEA FOR 8

- Taco Dogs
- Seedless purple grapes
- Chocolate chip cookies

GROCERIES NEEDED

Check staples: salsa

- 8 beef franks
- 1 (16-oz.) can refried beans
- 1 cup (4 oz.) shredded Cheddar cheese
- 8 (8-inch) flour tortillas
- 1 head curly lettuce
- 1 tomato
- 2 lb. seedless purple grapes
- 1 package chocolate chip cookies

PER ENTRÉE SERVING:
CALORIES 349 (56% from fat); FAT 21.8g (sat 9.8g, mono 8.2g, poly 0.8g); PROTEIN 15.8g; CARB 24g; FIBER 4.2g; CHOL 43mg; IRON 1.4mg; SODIUM 775mg; CALC 125mg

Prep: 5 min. ❋ **Cook:** 8 min.

Taco Dogs

Makes 8 servings

"I set up an assembly line with the ingredients for my 5-year-old grandson. Kids will love this because it's easy and they can make them all by themselves."—Rhonda F., West Liberty, KY

8 beef franks

1 cup refried beans
1 cup (4 oz.) shredded Cheddar cheese
½ cup salsa

8 (8-inch) flour tortillas
8 curly lettuce leaves
1 tomato, chopped

1. Cook franks in boiling water to cover 5 minutes; drain.

2. Combine beans, cheese, and salsa in a glass bowl; microwave at HIGH 2 minutes or until thoroughly heated, stirring once.

3. Spread bean mixture evenly on 1 side of each tortilla; top with lettuce and tomato. Place franks on tortillas, and roll up.

Nutrition Note: Our recipe was analyzed using an all-beef frank. Healthier alternatives, like reduced-fat beef franks or regular turkey franks, will save as much as 50 calories and 7 grams of fat per serving.

MENU IDEA FOR 4

- Pizza Bread Rollups
- Carrot and celery sticks with Ranch dressing

GROCERIES NEEDED

Check staples: large egg, dried Italian seasoning, Ranch dressing

- 1 (13.8-oz.) can refrigerated pizza crust dough (we tested with Pillsbury)
- 1 cup (4 oz.) shredded sharp Cheddar cheese
- 1 (3.5-oz.) package sliced turkey pepperoni
- 1 small jar pizza sauce
- 1 (8-oz.) bag carrots
- 1 bunch celery

PER ENTRÉE SERVING:
CALORIES 404 (35% from fat); FAT 15.5g (sat 7.7g, mono 1.5g, poly 0.9g); PROTEIN 21.5g; CARB 45g; FIBER 1.5g; CHOL 108mg; IRON 3.1mg; SODIUM 1464mg; CALC 213mg

Prep: 10 min. ❋ **Cook:** 35 min.

Pizza Bread Rollups

Makes 4 servings

"You'll be surprised how easy this is to make. My family thought it had the same great taste as pizza from a restaurant, and it looks more interesting."—Melanie R., Helena, AL

1 (13.8-oz.) can refrigerated pizza crust dough
1 large egg, lightly beaten
1 cup (4 oz.) shredded sharp Cheddar cheese
1 (3.5-oz.) package sliced turkey pepperoni
1 tsp. dried Italian seasoning

¾ cup pizza sauce

1. Preheat oven to 375°. Unroll dough onto a lightly greased jelly-roll pan, and pat or roll to ¼-inch thickness. Brush lightly with egg. Sprinkle with cheese and pepperoni. Roll up, jelly-roll fashion, pinching ends and seams to seal. Curl dough into a circle, pinching ends together to seal. Brush with egg, and sprinkle with Italian seasoning.

2. Bake at 375° for 30 to 35 minutes or until golden. Cut into 2-inch-thick slices, and serve with pizza sauce.

Flavor Change: To vary this recipe, use Canadian bacon and mozzarella cheese.

Get the Family Involved: Let the kids "paint" the beaten egg over the dough with a pastry brush.

Prep: 5 min. ✳ **Cook:** 10 min.

Ranch Noodles with Ham

Makes 6 servings

"Here's a preparation tip: This recipe is best served immediately and it's very quick. Make sure to prepare the side dish before you even get started!"—Kimberly B., Conway, SC

MENU IDEA FOR 6

- Ranch Noodles with Ham
- Steamed broccoli

GROCERIES NEEDED

Check staples: butter, Ranch dressing, grated Parmesan cheese

- 1 (12-oz.) package egg noodles
- 1 cup diced lean ham
- 1 (8-oz.) container reduced-fat sour cream
- 1¹/₂ lb. fresh broccoli

PER ENTRÉE SERVING:
CALORIES 460 (53% from fat); FAT 27.3g (sat 10.4g, mono 5g, poly 1.4g); PROTEIN 16.4g; CARB 36.8g; FIBER 1.7g; CHOL 100mg; IRON 2.4mg; SODIUM 667mg; CALC 121mg

1 (12-oz.) package egg noodles

1 cup diced lean ham

¹/₄ cup butter or margarine
¹/₂ cup reduced-fat sour cream
¹/₂ cup Ranch dressing
¹/₂ cup grated Parmesan cheese

1. Cook egg noodles according to package directions; drain and return to pot.

2. Meanwhile, sauté ham in a lightly greased skillet over medium-high heat 5 minutes or until crisp and fragrant. Set aside.

3. Add butter and remaining ingredients to noodles, stirring to blend. Divide mixture evenly among 6 serving dishes, and top with ham.

Health Note: Substituting light Ranch dressing for regular saves 7 grams of fat and 60 calories per serving.

MENU IDEA FOR 6
- Baked Apple French Toast
- Crisp bacon

GROCERIES NEEDED

Check staples: brown sugar, large eggs, milk, vanilla extract, ground cinnamon (optional)

- 2 (12-oz.) packages frozen, cooked apples (we tested with Stouffer's Harvest Apples)
- 1 (16-oz.) French bread loaf
- 1 small container frozen whipped topping (optional)
- 1 small jar cinnamon sticks (optional)
- 12 fully cooked bacon slices (such as Ready Crisp)

PER ENTRÉE SERVING:
CALORIES 366 (20% from fat); FAT 8.2g (sat 2.4g, mono 1.7g, poly 0.6g); PROTEIN 9.6g; CARB 61.6g; FIBER 2.4g; CHOL 146mg; IRON 1.9mg; SODIUM 315mg; CALC 109mg

Prep: 15 min. ✳ **Cook:** 47 min.

Baked Apple French Toast

Makes 6 servings

"There's something about breakfast foods that bring a certain comfort to hectic days. I count on this recipe to do just that. It's not fussy or complicated to assemble. And the result is golden brown French toast smothered in a syrupy apple topping that bakes in the same dish. It's a happy way to end the day."—Casey P., Auburn, AL

2 (12-oz.) packages frozen, cooked apples
½ (16-oz.) French bread loaf

⅓ cup firmly packed brown sugar

4 large eggs
1⅓ cups milk
1 tsp. vanilla extract

Garnishes: whipped topping, ground cinnamon, cinnamon sticks

1. Preheat oven to 350°. Thaw apples in microwave at MEDIUM (50% power) 6 to 7 minutes. Meanwhile, cut bread into 6 equal slices. Set aside.

2. Stir together apples and brown sugar. Spoon into a lightly greased 13- x 9-inch baking dish.

3. Whisk together eggs, milk, and vanilla in a large shallow dish until blended. Place bread slices, 1 at a time, in egg mixture, and let stand 1 minute. Turn bread slices over, and let stand 1 more minute. Place bread slices in an even layer on top of apple mixture.

4. Bake, uncovered, at 350° for 35 to 40 minutes or until bread centers are firm. Place each slice of French toast on individual plates, and spoon apple mixture over each. Garnish, if desired.

Note About Leftovers: Use the leftover French bread to make garlic bread, cheese toast, or croutons for another meal.

Bacon 'n' Egg Breakfast Empanadas

Makes 8 servings

"These hearty turnovers have made me a heroine in my son's eyes. If there are any leftovers, I refrigerate them in zip-top freezer bags. Reheat them in the microwave at MEDIUM for 1 minute or until thoroughly heated." —Katherine G., Vestavia Hills, AL

<table>
<tr><td>½</td><td>(8-oz.) package cream cheese, softened</td></tr>
<tr><td>½</td><td>cup (2 oz.) shredded sharp Cheddar cheese</td></tr>
<tr><td>1½</td><td>tsp. dried parsley flakes</td></tr>
<tr><td>½</td><td>tsp. seasoned salt</td></tr>
<tr><td>¼</td><td>tsp. pepper</td></tr>
<tr><td></td><td></td></tr>
<tr><td>1</td><td>Tbsp. butter or margarine</td></tr>
<tr><td>5</td><td>large eggs, beaten</td></tr>
<tr><td></td><td></td></tr>
<tr><td>1</td><td>(17.3-oz.) can refrigerated jumbo flaky biscuits</td></tr>
<tr><td>8</td><td>fully cooked bacon slices, reheated and crumbled</td></tr>
<tr><td>1</td><td>egg white, lightly beaten</td></tr>
<tr><td>1</td><td>tsp. sesame seeds (optional)</td></tr>
</table>

1. Preheat oven to 375°. Stir together first 5 ingredients in a medium bowl until blended.

2. Melt butter in a 9-inch skillet over medium heat; add eggs, and cook, without stirring, until eggs begin to set on bottom. Draw a spatula across bottom of skillet to form large curds. Continue cooking until eggs are slightly thickened but still moist. (Do not stir constantly.) Remove from heat, and let cool.

3. Flatten biscuits into 5-inch circles. Spread cream cheese mixture over dough circles, leaving ½-inch border around edge. Top evenly with scrambled eggs and bacon. Fold circles in half over mixture, pinching edges to seal, and place 2 inches apart on a lightly greased baking sheet; press sealed edges with tines of a fork. Brush tops evenly with egg white. Sprinkle with sesame seeds, if desired.

4. Bake at 375° for 14 to 16 minutes or until golden brown. Cool on a wire rack.

MENU IDEA FOR 8

- Bacon 'n' Egg Breakfast Empanadas
- Apple and orange wedges

GROCERIES NEEDED

Check staples: dried parsley flakes, seasoned salt, pepper, butter, large eggs

- 1 (8-oz.) package cream cheese
- ½ cup (2 oz.) shredded sharp Cheddar cheese
- 1 (17.3-oz.) can refrigerated jumbo flaky biscuits
- 8 fully cooked bacon slices (we tested with Ready Crisp)
- 1 small jar sesame seeds (optional)
- 4 apples and 4 oranges

PER ENTRÉE SERVING:
CALORIES 362 (56% from fat); FAT 22.4g (sat 9.2g, mono 3g, poly 0.7g); PROTEIN 12.7g; CARB 26.1g; FIBER 1g; CHOL 163mg; IRON 2.2mg; SODIUM 892mg; CALC 80mg

MENU IDEA FOR 6

- Chiles Rellenos Quiche
- Fresh berries and melon balls
- Orange juice

GROCERIES NEEDED

Check staples: 2% reduced-fat milk, large eggs

- 2 (4-oz.) cans diced green chiles
- 2 cups (8 oz.) shredded sharp Cheddar cheese
- 1 cup (4 oz.) shredded Monterey Jack cheese with peppers
- 1 box all-purpose baking mix (we tested with Bisquick)
- 1 (16-oz.) container part-skim ricotta cheese
- 1 pt. fresh berries
- 1 honeydew melon
- $1/2$ gal. orange juice

PER ENTRÉE SERVING:
CALORIES 460 (58% from fat); FAT 29.8g (sat 17.2g, mono 1.9g, poly 0.6g); PROTEIN 27g; CARB 24g; FIBER 2g; CHOL 217mg; IRON 1.6mg; SODIUM 722mg; CALC 777mg

Prep: 12 min. ❉ **Cook:** 45 min. ❉ **Other:** 10 min.

Chiles Rellenos Quiche

Makes 6 servings

All the cheesy goodness of the popular breakfast pie without the hassle of a crust. Use plain Monterey Jack cheese if your family doesn't prefer the kick of the jalapeños.

2 (4-oz.) cans diced green chiles, drained
2 cups (8 oz.) shredded sharp Cheddar cheese
1 cup (4 oz.) shredded Monterey Jack cheese with peppers

2 cups 2% reduced-fat milk
1 cup all-purpose baking mix
4 large eggs, lightly beaten
1 cup part-skim ricotta cheese

1. Preheat oven to 350°. Sprinkle green chiles, Cheddar cheese, and Monterey Jack cheese evenly into a lightly greased 11- x 8-inch baking dish.

2. Beat milk, baking mix, and eggs at low speed with an electric mixer until smooth. Stir in ricotta cheese; pour mixture evenly over chiles and cheeses in baking dish.

3. Bake, uncovered, at 350° for 45 minutes or until a knife inserted in center comes out clean. Let stand 10 minutes before cutting.

MENU IDEA FOR 4

- Banana Pancakes with Peanut Butter and Jam
- Fresh strawberries

GROCERIES NEEDED

Check staples: large eggs, ground cinnamon, maple syrup, peanut butter

- 1 box all-purpose baking mix (we tested with Bisquick)
- 1 pt. buttermilk
- 2 bananas
- 1 small jar strawberry jam
- 1 pt. fresh strawberries

PER ENTRÉE SERVING:
CALORIES 674 (19% from fat); FAT 14.5g (sat 3.8g, mono 4.9g, poly 2.7g); PROTEIN 17.4g; CARB 128g; FIBER 5.6g; CHOL 119mg; IRON 3.9mg; SODIUM 779mg; CALC 369mg

Prep: 10 min. ❋ **Cook:** 16 min.

Banana Pancakes with Peanut Butter and Jam

Makes 4 servings

Kids will dig this twist on the ordinary a.m. pancake.

2 cups all-purpose baking mix
1 cup buttermilk
1 cup mashed banana
2 large eggs
1/2 tsp. ground cinnamon

3/4 cup maple syrup
1/4 cup peanut butter
1/2 cup strawberry jam or jelly

1. Whisk together first 5 ingredients in a large bowl just until dry ingredients are moistened.

2. Heat a large nonstick griddle or skillet over medium heat until hot. For each pancake, pour about 1/4 cup batter onto griddle. Cook pancakes until tops are covered with bubbles and edges look cooked; turn and cook other side.

3. Whisk together maple syrup and peanut butter until smooth. Stack 3 pancakes on each serving plate, spreading about 1 Tbsp. jam between layers; spread peanut butter syrup over top. Serve pancakes with remaining peanut butter syrup.

Preparation Tip: You'll know the griddle is hot and ready when a few drops of water sprinkled on it dance, sputter, and evaporate.

Prep: 10 min. ✳ **Cook:** 25 min.

Sausage-and-Scrambled Egg Pizza

Makes 8 servings

"We love upside down days! That means breakfast for dinner to my family. My kids prefer this unique breakfast recipe with spicy sausage."—Joanne W., Cincinnati, OH

1 (13.8-oz.) can refrigerated pizza crust dough

1 lb. mild or hot ground pork sausage

6 large eggs, lightly beaten
½ tsp. seasoned pepper

1 (16-oz.) jar salsa
1 (8-oz.) package shredded Mexican four-cheese blend
Sour cream (optional)

1. Preheat oven to 425°. Unroll dough, and press into a lightly greased 15- x 10-inch jelly-roll pan. Bake at 425° for 6 to 8 minutes or until partially baked. Remove from oven, and set aside.

2. Meanwhile, brown sausage in a large nonstick skillet, stirring until it crumbles and is no longer pink. Drain and pat dry with paper towels; set aside. Wipe skillet clean.

3. Whisk together eggs and seasoned pepper. Cook in skillet over medium heat, without stirring, until eggs begin to set on bottom. Draw a spatula across bottom of skillet to form large curds. Continue cooking until eggs are thickened but still moist. (Do not stir constantly.) Remove from heat.

4. Spread salsa evenly over partially baked crust; top with sausage, scrambled eggs, and cheese. Bake at 425° for 12 minutes or until crust is golden. Serve with sour cream, if desired.

MENU IDEA FOR 8

- Easy Hash Brown and Sausage Casserole
- Orange juice

GROCERIES NEEDED

Check staples: large eggs, milk, salt, pepper

- 1 lb. mild or hot ground pork sausage
- 1 small onion
- 1 bag frozen cubed hash browns
- 2 cups (8 oz.) shredded sharp Cheddar cheese
- 1 box all-purpose baking mix (we tested with Bisquick)
- 1 bunch fresh parsley (optional)
- $^1/_2$ gal. orange juice

PER ENTRÉE SERVING:
CALORIES 456 (58% from fat); FAT 29.3g (sat 13g, mono 8.4g, poly 2.6g); PROTEIN 23.4g; CARB 24.8g; FIBER 1.5g; CHOL 204mg; IRON 1.8mg; SODIUM 858mg; CALC 359mg

Prep: 15 min. ❋ **Cook:** 40 min. ❋ **Other:** 5 min.

Easy Hash Brown and Sausage Casserole

Makes 8 servings

Just the slightest sight of onions is a turn-off to some kids. Finely chopping them should be helpful. If you have a severe case, substitute $^1/_4$ tsp. onion powder.

1   lb. mild or hot ground pork sausage
$^1/_4$ cup chopped onion
2$^1/_2$ cups frozen cubed hash browns (do not thaw)

5   large eggs, lightly beaten
2   cups (8 oz.) shredded sharp Cheddar cheese
1$^3/_4$ cups milk
1   cup all-purpose baking mix
$^1/_4$ tsp. salt
$^1/_4$ tsp. pepper
Garnish: fresh parsley sprigs

1. Preheat oven to 350°. Brown sausage with onion in a large skillet over medium-high heat 5 minutes or until meat crumbles. Stir in hash browns, and cook, stirring occasionally, until sausage is no longer pink and potatoes are lightly browned. Drain mixture on paper towels; spoon into a lightly greased 13- x 9-inch baking dish.

2. Whisk together eggs and next 5 ingredients; pour evenly over sausage mixture, stirring well. Bake, uncovered, at 350° for 30 minutes or until a wooden pick inserted in the center comes out clean. Remove from oven, and let stand 5 minutes. Garnish, if desired.

MENU IDEA FOR 6

- Ham-and-Swiss Muffins
- Cantaloupe wedges
- Strawberry smoothie

GROCERIES NEEDED

Check staples: butter, milk, Dijon mustard, large egg

- 1 medium-size sweet onion
- 1 box all-purpose baking mix (we tested with Bisquick)
- 2 cups (8 oz.) shredded Swiss or Cheddar cheese
- 1 cup finely chopped cooked ham
- 1 small jar poppy seeds (optional)
- 1 cantaloupe
- 1 (10-oz.) package frozen strawberries in light syrup (such as Bird's Eye)
- 1 (32-oz.) container vanilla low-fat yogurt (such as Dannon)

PER MUFFIN: CALORIES 175 (50% from fat); FAT 9.7g (sat 5.6g, mono 1.2g, poly 0.2g); PROTEIN 9.6g; CARB 12.5g; FIBER 0.8g; CHOL 50mg; IRON 0.7mg; SODIUM 368mg; CALC 259mg

Prep: 15 min. ✳ **Cook:** 25 min. ✳ **Other:** 3 min.

Ham-and-Swiss Muffins

Makes 12 (3-inch) muffins

"There's no reason that a balanced supper has to look like a stereotypical meal. For a change of pace, my daughter and I cover our basic food groups by eating one of these cheesy muffins, some fruit, and a dairy-rich smoothie. I freeze any leftover muffins up to a month for other meals." —Emily P., graphic designer

3 Tbsp. butter or margarine
1 medium-size sweet onion, finely chopped

1½ cups all-purpose baking mix
2 cups (8 oz.) shredded Swiss or Cheddar cheese, divided

½ cup milk
2 Tbsp. Dijon mustard
1 large egg
1 cup finely chopped cooked ham
Poppy seeds (optional)

1. Preheat oven to 425°. Melt butter in a skillet over medium-high heat; add onion, and sauté 3 to 5 minutes or until tender.

2. Combine baking mix and half of cheese in a large bowl; make a well in center of mixture.

3. Whisk together milk, Dijon mustard, and egg; add to cheese mixture, stirring just until moistened. Stir in onion and ham. Spoon into lightly greased muffin pans, filling two-thirds full. Sprinkle with remaining 1 cup cheese and poppy seeds, if desired.

4. Bake at 425° for 20 minutes or until golden. Let stand 2 to 3 minutes before removing from pans.

Smoothie Note: To make strawberry smoothies, thaw frozen strawberries according to package directions. Combine the strawberries and juice with yogurt and a handful of ice in an electric blender. Process until smooth.

Prep: 15 min. ✳ **Cook:** 16 min.

Cinnamon Toast Flapjacks

Makes 4 servings

Most busy moms prefer the simplicity of a complete pancake mix that doesn't require eggs or oil. That's what we used here.

2 cups complete pancake mix
1½ cups water
1 tsp. vanilla extract
¼ tsp. ground cinnamon

2 Tbsp. butter or margarine, divided
2 Tbsp. vegetable oil, divided
8 cinnamon or raisin bread slices
2 bananas, sliced
¼ cup chopped pecans
Maple syrup
Garnish: fresh strawberries

1. Whisk together first 4 ingredients in a large bowl just until dry ingredients are moistened.

2. Melt ½ Tbsp. butter with ½ Tbsp. oil in a large skillet over medium heat. Dip 2 bread slices in batter; cook in skillet 2 minutes on each side or until golden. Repeat procedure with remaining butter, oil, bread slices, and batter. Serve with bananas, pecans, and maple syrup. Garnish, if desired.

MENU IDEA FOR 4
- Cinnamon Toast Flapjacks
- Canadian bacon
- Fresh strawberries

GROCERIES NEEDED

Check staples: vanilla extract, ground cinnamon, butter, vegetable oil

- 1 box complete pancake mix (we tested with Hungry Jack Extra-Light and Fluffy)
- 1 cinnamon or raisin bread loaf (such as Pepperidge Farm)
- 2 bananas
- 1 small package chopped pecans
- 1 bottle maple syrup
- 1 pt. fresh strawberries
- 8 slices Canadian bacon

PER ENTRÉE SERVING:
CALORIES 747 (31% from fat); FAT 25.4g (sat 5.8g, mono 9.8g, poly 4.9g); PROTEIN 13.3g; CARB 119.1g; FIBER 8.3g; CHOL 20mg; IRON 4.5mg; SODIUM 1138mg; CALC 263mg

Prep: 12 min. ❋ **Cook:** 20 min.

Ham-and-Cheese Oven French Toast

Makes 6 servings

Sandwiched between two baking sheets and baked in a hot oven, this savory French toast recipe cooks practically hands-free. Cut up the honeydew while French toast bakes.

12 sandwich bread slices
¼ cup prepared mustard
12 (1-oz.) baked ham slices
6 (1-oz.) Monterey Jack cheese slices

3 large eggs
½ cup milk

1. Preheat oven to 475°. Spread 1 side of each bread slice with mustard. Layer 6 bread slices, mustard side up, with 1 ham slice, 1 cheese slice, and another ham slice; top with remaining bread slices, mustard side down.

2. Whisk together eggs and milk in a shallow dish until blended. Dip each sandwich into egg mixture, coating both sides. Place sandwiches 2 inches apart on a greased baking sheet. Place another greased baking sheet, greased side down, on top of sandwiches.

3. Bake at 475° for 15 to 20 minutes or until golden. Serve immediately.

MENU IDEA FOR 5

- Cheddar Pancakes with Pears and Bacon
- Vanilla yogurt

GROCERIES NEEDED

Check staples: vanilla extract, ground nutmeg, butter, brown sugar

- 1 box complete pancake mix (we tested with Hungry Jack Extra-Light and Fluffy)
- 1 cup (4 oz.) shredded sharp Cheddar cheese
- 2 large pears
- 5 fully cooked bacon slices (we tested with Ready Crisp)
- 1 (32-oz.) container low-fat vanilla yogurt

PER ENTRÉE SERVING:
CALORIES 193 (33% from fat); FAT 7g (sat 3.6g, mono 1.8g, poly 0.2g); PROTEIN 6.2g; CARB 29g; FIBER 1.3g; CHOL 18mg; IRON 1mg; SODIUM 500mg; CALC 178mg

Prep: 10 min. ❄ **Cook:** 12 min.

Cheddar Pancakes with Pears and Bacon

Makes 5 servings

While the pancakes cook, sliced pears simmer in butter and brown sugar creating enough pan juices to drench the cheese pancakes. There's no need for additional pancake syrup.

2 cups complete pancake mix
1½ cups water
1 tsp. vanilla extract
¼ tsp. ground nutmeg
1 cup (4 oz.) shredded sharp Cheddar cheese

1 Tbsp. butter or margarine
2 large pears, peeled, cored, and sliced
3 Tbsp. brown sugar
5 fully cooked bacon slices, crumbled

1. Whisk together first 5 ingredients. For each pancake, pour about ¼ cup batter onto a hot, lightly greased griddle or non-stick skillet. Cook pancakes 2 minutes or until tops are covered with bubbles and edges look cooked; turn and cook other sides until done.

2. Meanwhile, melt butter in a large non-stick skillet over medium heat. Add pears and brown sugar. Cook, stirring occasionally, 8 minutes or until pears are tender. Serve pears and pan juices over pancakes, and sprinkle with bacon.

Prep: 20 min.

Club Wraps

Makes 4 servings

Sandwiches are often the answer for suppers on-the-go. Wrap these individually in plastic wrap for after the game or an impromptu picnic. If you leave out certain ingredients for picky eaters, mark the plastic wrap with a permanent marker.

¹/₂ cup creamy mustard-mayonnaise blend
4 (10-inch) flour tortillas

¹/₂ lb. thinly sliced smoked turkey
¹/₂ lb. thinly sliced honey ham
2 cups shredded iceberg lettuce
1 cup (4 oz.) shredded mozzarella or smoked provolone cheese
2 medium tomatoes, seeded and chopped
¹/₂ small red onion, diced
8 fully cooked bacon slices
¹/₂ tsp. pepper

1. Spread mustard-mayonnaise blend evenly over 1 side of each tortilla, leaving a ¹/₂-inch border.

2. Layer turkey and next 6 ingredients evenly over tortillas; sprinkle with pepper. Roll up tortillas; secure with wooden picks, and cut in half diagonally.

MENU IDEA FOR 5

- Creamy Pineapple-and-Turkey Rollups
- Fresh vegetables

GROCERIES NEEDED

- 1 loaf thinly sliced white bread
- 1 (8-oz.) container soft pineapple cream cheese
- 1 bag preshredded carrots
- 10 oz. thinly sliced smoked turkey or ham
- 1 bunch celery
- 1 (8-oz.) bag baby carrots

PER 4 ROLLUPS: CALORIES 318 (41% from fat); FAT 14.6g (sat 8.8g, mono 0.3g, poly 0.6g); PROTEIN 17.8g; CARB 28g; FIBER 1.6g; CHOL 61mg; IRON 1.9mg; SODIUM 774mg; CALC 124mg

Prep: 12 min.

Creamy Pineapple-and-Turkey Rollups

Makes 5 servings

Take these fun sandwiches outside on the patio or deck for a casual family meal. With little cleanup, there will be plenty of time for a leisurely walk around the neighborhood.

10 thin white bread slices, crusts removed
1 (8-oz.) container soft pineapple cream cheese
1 cup preshredded carrot
10 oz. thinly sliced smoked turkey or ham

1. Roll bread slices with a rolling pin to $\frac{1}{8}$-inch thickness. Spread cream cheese evenly on 1 side of each bread slice; sprinkle with carrots. Top evenly with turkey slices. Roll up slices tightly, jelly-roll fashion. Cut each roll in half, if desired.

Prep Note: A serrated knife works best to trim the crust from sandwich bread. To speed the process, stack 2 or 3 bread slices and use a gentle sawing motion to remove the crust.

MENU IDEA FOR 4

- Turkey, Bacon, and Havarti Sandwich
- Potato chips
- Dill pickle spears

GROCERIES NEEDED

- 1 (7-inch) round sour-dough bread loaf
- 1 small bottle balsamic vinaigrette
- 1/2 lb. thinly sliced smoked turkey
- 1 (12-oz.) jar roasted red bell peppers
- 6 (1-oz.) slices Havarti or Muenster cheese
- 4 fully cooked bacon slices
- Potato chips
- Dill pickle spears

PER WEDGE: CALORIES 610 (40% from fat); FAT 27.4g (sat 12.6g, mono 2.4g, poly 1g); PROTEIN 33.4g; CARB 56.3g; FIBER 3g; CHOL 85mg; IRON 3mg; SODIUM 1873mg; CALC 304mg

Prep: 20 min. ✳ **Other:** 1 hr.

Turkey, Bacon, and Havarti Sandwich

Makes 4 servings

"It was great to make this early in the day during my baby's nap. As it chilled, the flavors improved. By dinner, all I had to do was cut it. That's a huge plus with a baby."—Virginia C., Mountain Brook, AL

1 (7-inch) round sourdough bread loaf

1/4 cup balsamic vinaigrette
1/2 lb. thinly sliced smoked turkey
1 (12-oz.) jar roasted red bell peppers, drained and sliced
6 (1-oz.) slices Havarti or Muenster cheese
4 fully cooked bacon slices

1. Cut off top 2 inches of sourdough loaf, reserving top; hollow out loaf, leaving a 1-inch-thick shell. (Reserve soft center of bread loaf for another use, if desired.)

2. Drizzle 2 Tbsp. vinaigrette evenly in bottom bread shell; layer with half of turkey, peppers, and cheese. Repeat layers, and top with bacon. Drizzle evenly with remaining 2 Tbsp. vinaigrette. Cover with reserved bread top, pressing down firmly. Wrap in plastic wrap, and chill at least 1 hour or up to 8 hours before serving. Cut into 4 wedges.

MENU IDEA FOR 4

- Philly Cheesesteaks
- Broccoli florets and Ranch dressing

GROCERIES NEEDED

Check staples: olive oil, bottled minced garlic, sugar, dried oregano, white wine vinegar, salt, Ranch dressing

- 1 large onion
- 1 small red bell pepper
- 1 small green bell pepper
- 4 oz. processed cheese (we tested with Velveeta)
- ³/₄ lb. thinly sliced roast beef
- 1 can beef broth or 1 jar beef bouillon
- 1 package hot dog buns
- 1 lb. broccoli florets

PER SANDWICH: CALORIES 374 (35% from fat); FAT 14.5g (sat 6.1g, mono 4.1g, poly 0.9g); PROTEIN 25g; CARB 36.2g; FIBER 2.7g; CHOL 51mg; IRON 2.9mg; SODIUM 1488mg; CALC 204mg

Prep: 10 min. ✳ **Cook:** 15 min.

Philly Cheesesteaks

Makes 4 servings

Offer plenty of napkins with this deliciously messy sandwich. It consists of thinly sliced roast beef and sautéed onions smothered in cheese and served on a bun.

1 Tbsp. olive oil
1 large onion, thinly sliced
1 small red bell pepper, sliced into thin strips
1 small green bell pepper, sliced into thin strips
2 tsp. bottled minced garlic

2 tsp. sugar
1 tsp. dried oregano
2 tsp. white wine vinegar
¼ tsp. salt
4 oz. processed cheese, cubed

³/₄ lb. thinly sliced roast beef, shredded
3 Tbsp. beef broth

4 hot dog buns, toasted

1. Heat oil in a large nonstick skillet over medium-high heat. Add onion, bell peppers, and garlic; sauté 4 minutes or until tender. Reduce heat; cook 8 minutes or until tender, stirring occasionally.

2. Stir in sugar, oregano, vinegar, salt, and cheese; cook 2 minutes or until cheese melts, stirring constantly.

3. Combine beef and broth in a microwave-safe bowl. Cover and microwave at HIGH 2 minutes or until hot.

4. Divide beef mixture evenly among buns; top each with cheese mixture.

MENU IDEA FOR 4

- Sticky Finger Sandwiches
- Baked potato chips

GROCERIES NEEDED

Check staples: peanut butter, honey

- 1 loaf cinnamon-swirl, raisin, or banana bread
- 1 large banana
- 1 can sweetened coconut
- Baked potato chips

PER SANDWICH: CALORIES 356 (39% from fat); FAT 15.3g (sat 4.1g, mono 4g, poly 2.2g); PROTEIN 11.1g; CARB 46.4g; FIBER 6.1g; CHOL 0mg; IRON 2.1mg; SODIUM 345mg; CALC 8mg

Prep: 10 min.

Sticky Finger Sandwiches

Makes 4 servings

"My kids signaled me with two thumbs up after trying these unique peanut butter sandwiches. And they couldn't be easier to make. Practically all of the ingredients are things that we keep in our kitchen on a regular basis. We also like them with crunchy peanut butter and on toasted bread."—Anne M., Marietta, GA

¼ cup peanut butter
8 (½-inch-thick) slices cinnamon swirl, raisin, or banana bread
½ large banana, sliced
¼ cup toasted sweetened coconut
4 tsp. honey

1. Spread peanut butter evenly over 4 bread slices; top with banana and coconut. Drizzle with honey. Top with remaining bread slices. Cut each sandwich into quarters.

MENU IDEA FOR 4

- Southern Reuben Melts
- Potato chips
- Dill pickle spears

GROCERIES NEEDED

Check staples: mayonnaise, ketchup, ground red pepper, butter-flavored cooking spray

- 1 small jar sweet pickle relish
- 1 (16-oz.) bag fresh coleslaw mix (we tested with Fresh Express)
- 1 loaf rye or whole wheat bread
- 1 (6-oz.) package Swiss cheese slices
- 12 oz. thinly sliced ham
- Potato chips
- Dill pickle spears

PER SANDWICH: CALORIES 829 (65% from fat); FAT 59.9g (sat 14.7g, mono 3.9g, poly 0.9g); PROTEIN 31.2g; CARB 38g; FIBER 4.4g; CHOL 97mg; IRON 2.3mg; SODIUM 1668mg; CALC 453mg

Prep: 16 min. ✳ **Cook:** 15 min.

Southern Reuben Melts

Makes 4 servings

Thinly sliced ham and coleslaw stand in for corned beef and sauerkraut to give this Reuben melt a Southern accent. The portion size is generous, so count on it to satisfy the ravenous appetites of teenagers.

1 cup mayonnaise
¼ cup ketchup
1 to 2 Tbsp. sweet pickle relish
⅛ tsp. ground red pepper
3 cups coleslaw mix
8 rye or whole wheat bread slices
1 (6-oz.) package Swiss cheese slices
12 oz. thinly sliced ham

Butter-flavored cooking spray

1. Preheat oven to 375°. Stir together first 4 ingredients. Combine coleslaw mix and ½ cup mayonnaise mixture in a medium bowl. Spread 1 Tbsp. remaining mayonnaise mixture evenly on 1 side of each bread slice. Layer 4 bread slices, mayonnaise sides up, with cheese, ham, and coleslaw mixture. Top with remaining bread slices, mayonnaise side down.

2. Place sandwiches 2 inches apart on a baking sheet generously coated with cooking spray. Place another baking sheet generously coated with cooking spray, greased-side down, on sandwiches.

3. Bake at 375° for 10 to 15 minutes or until golden.

MENU IDEA FOR 4

- Toasted Cream Cheese-and-Apple Pockets
- Sausage links
- Orange wedges

GROCERIES NEEDED

Check staples: powdered sugar, ground cinnamon, butter, granulated sugar

- 2 loaves fresh whole wheat bread
- 1 (8-oz.) package reduced-fat cream cheese
- 1 Golden Delicious apple
- 8 sausage links
- 4 oranges

PER 4 POCKETS: CALORIES 434 (32% from fat); FAT 15.5g (sat 8.8g, mono 2.3g, poly 1g); PROTEIN 14.3g; CARB 63.4g; FIBER 6.7g; CHOL 34mg; IRON 3.1mg; SODIUM 765mg; CALC 140mg

Prep: 25 min. ✳ **Cook:** 10 min.

Toasted Cream Cheese-and-Apple Pockets

Makes 4 servings

Toasted whole wheat bread pockets have a cinnamony crust and a surprise apple filling. Serve them warm or at room temperature.

32 fresh whole wheat bread slices

1 (8-oz.) package reduced-fat cream cheese, softened
1 Golden Delicious apple, peeled and diced
¼ cup powdered sugar
¼ tsp. ground cinnamon, divided
1 Tbsp. butter or margarine, melted
2 Tbsp. granulated sugar

1. Preheat oven to 400°. Cut out centers of each bread slice with a 3-inch round cutter. (Reserve scraps for another use, if desired.) Place half of bread rounds on a lightly greased baking sheet.

2. Stir together cream cheese, apple, powdered sugar, and ⅛ tsp. cinnamon until blended. Spoon about 1 Tbsp. apple mixture onto center of each bread round on baking sheet; top with remaining bread rounds. Crimp edges with a fork to seal; brush tops with butter. Stir together remaining ⅛ tsp. cinnamon and 2 Tbsp. sugar; sprinkle over sandwiches.

3. Bake at 400° for 8 to 10 minutes or until golden.

Leftover Note: Store any leftovers in an airtight container in the freezer for up to 1 month. To reheat for a quick afternoon snack, wrap each frozen sandwich in a paper towel, and microwave at HIGH for 45 seconds or until warm.

MENU IDEA FOR 4

- Grilled Peanut Butter and Banana Split Sandwiches
- Rainbow sherbet

GROCERIES NEEDED

Check staples: butter, peanut butter, honey

- 2 small bananas
- 1 loaf firm white sandwich bread
- 1 (6-oz.) package semisweet chocolate mini-morsels
- 1 small container fresh strawberries
- 1 small jar pineapple jam
- ¹/₂ gal. rainbow sherbet

PER SANDWICH: CALORIES 398 (32% from fat); FAT 14.3g (sat 4.7g, mono 5.4g, poly 3.2g); PROTEIN 9.2g; CARB 61.9g; FIBER 4.2g; CHOL 10mg; IRON 2.7mg; SODIUM 489mg; CALC 100mg

Prep: 15 min. ☀ **Cook:** 8 min.

Grilled Peanut Butter and Banana Split Sandwiches

Makes 4 servings

From time to time, supper just needs to be a little zany and a bit indulgent. Surprise your crew with these fun sandwiches, and watch for smiles.

2 small bananas, cut in half crosswise
4 tsp. butter or margarine, softened
8 (1-oz.) slices firm white sandwich bread, divided
¹/₄ cup creamy peanut butter
2 tsp. honey
2 tsp. semisweet chocolate mini-morsels
4 large strawberries, thinly sliced
¹/₄ cup pineapple jam

1. Cut each banana half lengthwise into 3 slices. Spread ¹/₂ tsp. butter on 1 side of each bread slice. Combine peanut butter and honey; spread over plain side of 4 bread slices. Sprinkle each slice with ¹/₂ tsp. chocolate morsels; top evenly with strawberry and banana slices. Spread remaining bread slices with pineapple jam. Place on top of sandwiches, jam sides down.

2. Heat a large nonstick skillet over medium-high heat. Add 2 sandwiches; cook 2 minutes on each side or until lightly browned. Repeat procedure with remaining 2 sandwiches.

MENU IDEA FOR 4

- Sausage and Pepper Subs
- Green seedless grapes

GROCERIES NEEDED

Check staples: olive oil, bottled minced garlic, fennel seeds, balsamic vinegar

- 12 oz. sweet Italian turkey sausage links
- 1 (1-lb.) bag frozen bell pepper stir-fry (we tested with Bird's Eye)
- 1 (12-oz.) jar marinara sauce
- 4 (2½-oz.) hoagie rolls
- 1 lb. green seedless grapes

PER SANDWICH: CALORIES 403 (30% from fat); FAT 13.4g (sat 3.6g, mono 3.8g, poly 2.6g); PROTEIN 24.6g; CARB 49.6g; FIBER 3.8g; CHOL 72mg; IRON 4.3mg; SODIUM 1296mg; CALC 71mg

Prep: 10 min. ❋ **Cook:** 12½ min.

Sausage and Pepper Subs

Makes 4 servings

These sandwiches use thick slices of turkey sausage links instead of fussy meatballs. The filling is generous, so consider serving the sandwiches with a knife and fork.

1 tsp. olive oil
12 oz. sweet Italian turkey sausage links, cut into ½-inch pieces
2 tsp. bottled minced garlic
¼ tsp. fennel seeds, crushed
3 cups frozen bell pepper stir-fry, thawed
1 (12-oz.) jar marinara sauce
1 tsp. balsamic vinegar

4 (2½-oz.) hoagie rolls, split lengthwise

1. Heat oil in a large nonstick skillet over medium-high heat. Add sausage, and cook 7 minutes or until lightly browned, stirring occasionally. Add garlic and fennel to pan; cook 30 seconds, stirring constantly. Stir in bell pepper stir-fry and marinara sauce; bring to a boil. Reduce heat, and simmer 5 minutes. Stir in vinegar.

2. Spoon about 1 cup sausage mixture into each hoagie roll.

MENU IDEA FOR 4

- Monte Cristo Sandwiches
- Baked potato chips

GROCERIES NEEDED

Check staples: honey mustard, milk, large eggs, vegetable cooking spray, powdered sugar

- 1 loaf white bread
- 1/2 lb. thinly sliced smoked ham
- 4 (1-oz.) slices Swiss cheese
- 1 jar seedless raspberry jam
- 1 bag baked potato chips

PER SANDWICH: CALORIES 419 (27% from fat); FAT 12.7g (sat 6.4g, mono 2.6g, poly 1.1g); PROTEIN 24.4g; CARB 52.4g; FIBER 1.6g; CHOL 58mg; IRON 2.8mg; SODIUM 1021mg; CALC 388mg

Prep: 10 min. ✳ **Cook:** 12 min.

Monte Cristo Sandwiches

Makes 4 servings

The characteristic sweet-and-savory flavors of this classic diner sandwich will wow your family. Strawberry jam or maple syrup stand in nicely for the raspberry jam.

3 Tbsp. honey mustard
8 (1-oz.) slices white bread
1/2 lb. thinly sliced smoked ham
4 (1-oz.) slices Swiss cheese

1/3 cup milk
2 large egg whites

Vegetable cooking spray
2 tsp. powdered sugar
1/4 cup seedless raspberry jam

1. Spread about 1 tsp. mustard on 1 side of each bread slice. Layer 4 bread slices, mustard side up, with ham and cheese. Cover with the remaining 4 bread slices, mustard sides down.

2. Whisk together milk and egg whites in a shallow dish until blended. Dip each sandwich into milk mixture, coating both sides.

3. Heat a large nonstick skillet coated with cooking spray over medium heat. Add 2 sandwiches, and cook 3 minutes on each side or until lightly browned. Repeat procedure with remaining sandwiches. Sprinkle each sandwich with 1/2 tsp. sugar, and serve with jam.

Make-Ahead Meals

Big Batch Soups • Freezer Pleasers
Double-Duty Meals

Prep: 12 min. ❋ **Cook:** 35 min.

Loaded Potato Soup

Makes 13 cups

"With two teenagers involved in several time-consuming activities, Monday is the only night of the week I can bank on my entire family for dinner. This is one of their favorite soups, so I seize the chance with them all at the table and serve something they love. After dinner, we pack up the leftovers in single servings for lunches or evenings when our schedules don't mesh."—Elizabeth T., Foods Editor

MENU IDEA FOR 10

- Loaded Potato Soup
- Breadsticks

GROCERIES NEEDED

Check staples: butter, all-purpose flour, milk, salt, ground white pepper

- 5 large baking potatoes (about 4^1/$_2$ lb.)
- 1 medium onion
- 1 qt. half-and-half
- 1^1/$_4$ cups (5 oz.) shredded Cheddar cheese
- 8 fully cooked bacon slices
- 1 bunch green onions
- Breadsticks

PER 1^1/$_3$ CUPS SOUP:
CALORIES 421 (52% from fat); FAT 24.1g (sat 14.7g, mono 6.3g, poly 0.9g); PROTEIN 13g; CARB 39g; FIBER 2.3g; CHOL 74mg; IRON 0.9mg; SODIUM 491mg; CALC 301mg

5 large baking potatoes

^{1}/$_4$ cup butter or margarine
1 medium onion, chopped
^{1}/$_3$ cup all-purpose flour
1 qt. half-and-half
3 cups milk
1 tsp. salt
^{1}/$_8$ tsp. ground white pepper

1^1/$_4$ cups (5 oz.) shredded Cheddar cheese
8 fully cooked bacon slices, crumbled
Garnish: sliced green onions

1. Prick each potato several times with a fork. Arrange potatoes 1 inch apart in microwave on paper towels. Microwave at HIGH about 20 minutes, turning and rearranging after 10 minutes. Let cool.

2. Peel potatoes, and coarsely mash with a fork.

3. Melt butter in a Dutch oven over medium heat; add onion, and sauté until tender. Add flour, stirring until smooth. Stir in potatoes, half-and-half, and next 3 ingredients; cook over low heat about 15 minutes or until thoroughly heated.

4. Top each serving with cheese and bacon. Garnish, if desired.

Storage Note: Refrigerate leftovers in an airtight container up to 3 days.

GROCERIES NEEDED

Check staples:
Vegetable cooking spray, bottled minced garlic, olive oil, dried basil, dried oregano, pepper, grated Parmesan cheese (optional)

- 1 lb. extra-lean ground beef

- 3 oz. sliced turkey pepperoni

- 1 (8-oz.) package sliced fresh mushrooms

- 1 green bell pepper

- 1 bunch green onions

- 1 (28-oz.) can crushed tomatoes

- 1 (32-oz.) container chicken broth

- 1 (4¹/₂-oz.) tube tomato paste

- 1 bunch fresh basil (optional)

- Italian bread

PER 1²/₃ CUPS SOUP:
CALORIES 266 (37% from fat);
FAT 10.8g (sat 3.3g, mono 4.1g,
poly 0.8g); PROTEIN 24.8g;
CARB 15.8g; FIBER 4g;
CHOL 52mg; IRON 4.4mg;
SODIUM 1561mg; CALC 86mg

Prep: 25 min. ❊ **Cook:** 45 min.

Italian-Style Beef-and-Pepperoni Soup

Makes 10 cups

"My 8-year-old requests seconds and eats every drop. Like so many soups, it's even better the second time around."—Karen I., Corinth, MS

1 lb. extra-lean ground beef
3 oz. sliced turkey pepperoni
Vegetable cooking spray

1 cup sliced fresh mushrooms
1 green bell pepper, chopped
1 bunch green onions, chopped
1 tsp. bottled minced garlic
1 tsp. olive oil

1 (28-oz.) can crushed tomatoes
1 (32-oz.) container chicken broth
2 Tbsp. tomato paste
1 tsp. dried basil or 1 Tbsp. chopped fresh basil
1 tsp. dried oregano or 1 Tbsp. chopped fresh oregano
1 tsp. ground pepper
Garnishes: grated Parmesan cheese, sliced fresh basil

1. Cook ground beef and pepperoni in a Dutch oven coated with cooking spray over medium-high heat, stirring until beef crumbles and is no longer pink. Drain and pat dry with paper towels. Wipe Dutch oven clean.

2. Sauté mushrooms and next 3 ingredients in hot oil in Dutch oven 5 minutes.

3. Stir in beef mixture, crushed tomatoes, and next 5 ingredients. Bring to a boil; reduce heat, and simmer 30 minutes. Garnish, if desired.

Storage Note: Refrigerate leftovers in an airtight container up to 3 days, or freeze up to 1 month.

MENU IDEA FOR 8

- Chunky Steak and Vegetable Soup
- Whole grain crackers

GROCERIES NEEDED

Check staples: all-purpose flour, vegetable oil, beef bouillon granules, pepper

- 2 lb. top round steak
- 5 small baking potatoes
- 3 carrots
- 2 small onions
- 1 bunch celery
- 1 (6-oz.) can tomato paste
- 1 (10-oz.) package frozen sweet peas
- 1 (16-oz.) can whole kernel corn
- 1 box whole grain crackers

PER 2 CUPS SOUP: CALORIES 442 (30% from fat); FAT 14.8g (sat 4.2g, mono 6.2g, poly 2.7g); PROTEIN 30.4g; CARB 45.8g; FIBER 6.2g; CHOL 46mg; IRON 4.5mg; SODIUM 549mg; CALC 54mg

Prep: 15 min. ❊ **Cook:** 8 hrs., 36 min.

Chunky Steak and Vegetable Soup

Makes 16 cups

This slow-cooked meal makes a lot so it's perfect when friends stay over unexpectedly for supper. Adding the peas and corn toward the end of cooking keeps them from getting too soft.

2 lb. top round steak, cut into 1-inch cubes
⅓ cup all-purpose flour
3 Tbsp. vegetable oil

6 cups water
5 small baking potatoes, cut into ½-inch cubes
3 carrots, sliced
2 small onions, chopped
1 celery rib, chopped
1 (6-oz.) can tomato paste
2 Tbsp. beef bouillon granules
1 to 2 tsp. pepper

1 cup frozen sweet peas, thawed
1 (16-oz.) can whole kernel corn, drained

1. Place steak in a zip-top freezer bag; add flour, and toss to coat. Brown steak in hot oil in a large skillet over medium-high heat 5 to 6 minutes or until browned. Drain well.

2. Combine steak, 6 cups water, and next 7 ingredients in a 7-qt. slow cooker. Cover and cook on HIGH 8 hours.

3. Stir in peas and corn; cover and cook on HIGH 30 more minutes.

Storage Note: Refrigerate leftovers in an airtight container up to 4 days. Add water to thin soup when reheating, if necessary. (This soup does not freeze well.)

Broccoli, Ham, and Cheese Soup

Makes 12 cups

This decadent soup will have your children happily eating their broccoli. We pureed half the soup to make a thicker consistency. If you prefer a chunkier soup, don't puree it.

5 large baking potatoes, peeled and cubed
1 medium onion, chopped
2 (14-oz.) cans chicken broth
1 (12-oz.) package diced cooked ham
1½ cups broccoli florets
2 tsp. bottled minced garlic
½ tsp. salt
¾ tsp. pepper

2 cups whipping cream
2 cups (8 oz.) shredded sharp Cheddar cheese
Shredded Cheddar cheese (optional)

1. Combine first 8 ingredients in a 5-qt. slow cooker. Cover and cook on HIGH 1 hour; reduce heat to LOW and cook 6 hours or until potatoes are tender.

2. Process half of soup mixture in a food processor until smooth. Return pureed soup, whipping cream, and 2 cups cheese to slow cooker. Cover and cook on LOW 30 more minutes or until thoroughly heated. Top with additional shredded Cheddar cheese, if desired.

Storage Note: Refrigerate leftovers in an airtight container up to 3 days, or freeze up to 1 month.

MENU IDEA FOR 8

- Broccoli, Ham, and Cheese Soup
- Crusty rolls

GROCERIES NEEDED

Check staples: bottled minced garlic, salt, pepper

- 5 large baking potatoes (about 4½ lb.)
- 1 medium onion
- 2 (14-oz.) cans chicken broth
- 1 (12-oz.) package diced cooked ham
- 1½ cups broccoli florets
- 2 cups whipping cream
- 2 cups (8 oz.) shredded sharp Cheddar cheese
- Additional shredded sharp Cheddar cheese (optional)
- 8 crusty rolls

PER 1½ CUPS SOUP:
CALORIES 580 (49% from fat); FAT 31.7g (sat 18.6g, mono 0.8g, poly 0.3g); PROTEIN 19.3g; CARB 53.7g; FIBER 3.7g; CHOL 131mg; IRON 1.3mg; SODIUM 1425mg; CALC 222mg

MENU IDEA FOR 8

- Cowboy Chili
- Baked tortilla chips

GROCERIES NEEDED

Check staples: chili powder, pepper

- 1 lb. ground pork sausage
- 1 large onion
- 4 (16-oz.) cans dark red kidney beans
- 4 (14.5-oz.) cans chili-style diced tomatoes
- 3 (8-oz.) cans tomato sauce
- 2 (11-oz.) cans Mexican-style corn
- Baked tortilla chips

PER 2 CUPS SOUP: CALORIES 450 (33% from fat); FAT 16.5g (sat 5.1g, mono 6.9g, poly 2.3g); PROTEIN 21.9g; CARB 56.4g; FIBER 13.1g; CHOL 41mg; IRON 4.3mg; SODIUM 2321mg; CALC 129mg

Prep: 5 min. ❋ **Cook:** 43 min.

Cowboy Chili

Makes 16 cups

It won't take long to rustle up the kids for a bowl of this hearty chili. It's not spicy so serve it with hot sauce if you like. Leftovers are great spooned into a hot, buttered baked potato. Kids might prefer turning it into a chili-cheese dog.

1 lb. ground pork sausage
1 large onion, chopped

4 (16-oz.) cans dark red kidney beans, drained and rinsed
4 (14.5-oz.) cans chili-style diced tomatoes
3 (8-oz.) cans tomato sauce
2 (11-oz.) cans Mexican-style corn, drained
3 Tbsp. chili powder
1 tsp. pepper

1. Cook sausage and onion in a Dutch oven over medium-high heat, stirring until meat crumbles and is no longer pink. Drain and pat dry with paper towels. Wipe Dutch oven clean, and return sausage mixture to pan.

2. Stir beans and remaining 5 ingredients into sausage mixture. Bring to a boil; cover, reduce heat, and simmer 30 minutes.

Storage Note: Refrigerate leftovers in an airtight container up to 4 days, or freeze up to 1 month.

Nutrition Note: Wiping out the Dutch oven with paper towels after cooking the sausage is a great way to eliminate unnecessary fat.

MENU IDEA FOR 12

- Easy Cheesy Kielbasa with Beans
- Corn sticks or muffins
- Slaw

GROCERIES NEEDED

Check staples: pepper

- 1 lb. ground chuck
- 1 large green bell pepper
- 1 large onion
- 1 lb. kielbasa or smoked sausage
- 4 (16-oz.) cans pinto beans
- 4 (15-oz.) cans pork and beans
- 2 (10³/₄-oz.) cans tomato soup
- 1 (14¹/₂-oz.) can diced tomatoes
- 1 (10-oz.) can diced tomato and green chiles
- 2 cups (8 oz.) shredded Cheddar cheese
- 12 deli corn muffins
- 3 pt. deli slaw

PER 1²/₃ CUPS SOUP:
CALORIES 593 (38% from fat);
FAT 25.2g (sat 10.6g, mono 10g,
poly 1.6g); PROTEIN 31.2g;
CARB 61g; FIBER 15.2g;
CHOL 72mg; IRON 6.2mg;
SODIUM 1895mg; CALC 264mg

Prep: 10 min. ✳ **Cook:** 45 min.

Easy Cheesy Kielbasa with Beans

Makes 20 cups

"If I know a full day of errands is going to keep me away from home until late in the day, I make this recipe in the slow cooker. I prepare it early in the morning, through Step 1, and transfer the sausage and ground chuck mixture to a 6-qt. slow cooker. I'll add the remaining ingredients except the cheese, and cook on low for 8 hours. I come home to the most wonderful aroma, and all I have to do is stir in the cheese."—Lorene C., Columbus, GA

1 lb. ground chuck
1 large green bell pepper, diced
1 large onion, chopped
1 lb. kielbasa or smoked sausage, thinly sliced

4 (16-oz.) cans pinto beans, undrained
4 (15-oz.) cans pork and beans, undrained
2 (10³/₄-oz.) cans tomato soup
1 (14¹/₂-oz.) can diced tomatoes, undrained
1 (10-oz.) can diced tomato and green chiles, undrained
¹/₂ tsp. pepper
2 cups (8 oz.) shredded Cheddar cheese

1. Cook first 3 ingredients in a Dutch oven over medium-high heat, stirring until beef crumbles and is no longer pink. Remove from pot, and drain. Brown sausage in Dutch oven over medium-high heat; drain on paper towels, and wipe Dutch oven clean with a paper towel. Return sausage and ground chuck mixture to Dutch oven.

2. Stir in pinto beans and next 5 ingredients. Bring to a boil; reduce heat, and simmer, stirring occasionally, 30 minutes. Stir in cheese.

Storage Note: Refrigerate leftovers in an airtight container up to 3 days, or freeze up to 1 month.

MENU IDEA FOR 8

• Quick Shrimp
  Chowder

• Oyster crackers

GROCERIES NEEDED

Check staples: butter,
milk, ground red
pepper

• 1 medium onion

• 2 (10³/₄-oz.) cans
  cream of potato soup

• 1¹/₂ lb. medium-size
  frozen raw shrimp in
  shells

• 1 cup (4 oz.) shred-
  ded Monterey Jack
  cheese

• 1 bunch fresh parsley
  (optional)

• 1 package oyster
  crackers

PER 1¹/₄ CUPS SOUP:
CALORIES 300 (42% from fat);
FAT 14g (sat 8g, mono 3.1g,
poly 1g); PROTEIN 25.6g;
CARB 16.5g; FIBER 0.8g;
CHOL 166mg; IRON 2.4mg;
SODIUM 814mg; CALC 286mg

Prep: 15 min. ✳ **Cook:** 20 min.

Quick Shrimp Chowder

Makes 10 cups

"My kids call this a 'keeper' soup. I'll admit I was surprised
that most of this soup is made from store-bought soup and milk
and is still so yummy. I think sautéing the onions in butter is the
secret to making it taste homemade."—Monica B., Conway, SC

2 Tbsp. butter or margarine
1 medium onion, chopped

2 (10³/₄-oz.) cans cream of potato soup
3¹/₂ cups milk
¹/₄ tsp. ground red pepper
1¹/₂ lb. medium-size frozen raw shrimp in
   shells, peeled and deveined
1 cup (4 oz.) shredded Monterey Jack
   cheese
Garnish: chopped fresh parsley

1. Melt butter in a Dutch oven over
medium heat; add onion, and sauté until
tender.

2. Stir in cream of potato soup, milk, and
pepper; bring to a boil. Add shrimp;
reduce heat, and simmer, stirring often,
5 minutes or just until shrimp turn pink.
Stir in cheese until melted. Garnish, if
desired. Serve immediately.

Storage Note: Refrigerate leftovers in an airtight container up to 4 days, or freeze
up to 1 month.

Shopping Tip: Look for "easy peel" shrimp in your grocer's freezer section. The
shells have been pre-cut down the length of each shrimp, making it almost
effortless to slip off the peel and remove the vein, too.

Prep: 10 min. ✷ **Cook:** 8 hrs., 15 min.

Beans with Smoked Sausage

Makes 10 cups

"I used to think dried beans had to be soaked overnight before cooking. Honestly, after my kids are in bed, I'm exhausted and would just forget. This recipe is great. It's healthy and the beans don't have to soak."—Dorothy H., Huntsville, AL

MENU IDEA FOR 8

- Beans with Smoked Sausage
- Spinach salad with poppy seed dressing

GROCERIES NEEDED

Check staples: vegetable oil, bottled minced garlic, dried thyme, celery seeds, pepper

- 2 lb. smoked turkey sausage
- 1 small onion or 3 shallots
- 1 lb. dried navy, great Northern, or other dried white beans
- 2 (14.5-oz.) cans chicken broth
- Fresh thyme (optional)
- 1 (10-oz.) package fresh spinach
- Poppy seed dressing

PER 1¼ CUPS SOUP:
CALORIES 390 (34% from fat);
FAT 14.8g (sat 3.3g, mono 4.9g,
poly 4.2g); PROTEIN 27.6g;
CARB 36.9g; FIBER 13g;
CHOL 79mg; IRON 4.9mg;
SODIUM 1737mg; CALC 124mg

2 lb. smoked turkey sausage, cut into 1½-inch pieces
1 Tbsp. vegetable oil
⅓ cup minced onion or shallots
1½ tsp. bottled minced garlic

2 cups dried navy, great Northern, or other dried white beans
2 cups water
1 Tbsp. dried or ¼ cup minced fresh thyme
1 tsp. celery seeds
¼ tsp. pepper
2 (14.5-oz.) cans chicken broth
Garnish: fresh thyme sprigs

1. Brown sausage in a large skillet over medium-high heat; drain on paper towels. Add oil to skillet, and place over medium-high heat until hot. Add onion and garlic; sauté until tender.

2. Sort and wash beans. Combine sausage, onion, beans, water, and next 4 ingredients in a 5-qt. slow cooker. Cover and cook on HIGH 8 hours or until beans are tender. Garnish, if desired.

Storage Note: Refrigerate leftovers in an airtight container up to 5 days, or freeze up to 1 month.

Preparation Tip: To sort and wash beans, place them in a colander and rinse thoroughly under cold running water while removing any discolored beans or debris.

MENU IDEA FOR 6

- Mexican Lime-Chicken Soup
- Tortilla chips
- Chocolate chip cookies

GROCERIES NEEDED

Check staples: vegetable oil, bottled minced garlic, salt, pepper

- 1 large red bell pepper
- 1 large onion
- 2 (14.5-oz.) cans Mexican-style stewed tomatoes
- 2 limes
- 4 (14-oz.) cans chicken broth
- 3 cups chopped cooked chicken
- 1 bunch fresh cilantro
- 1 medium jalapeño pepper or pickled jalapeño pepper
- Shredded Cheddar cheese and sour cream (optional)
- Tortilla chips
- 1 package chocolate chip cookies

PER 2 CUPS SOUP: CALORIES 259 (42% from fat); FAT 12.1g (sat 1.9g, mono 3.8g, poly 3.2g); PROTEIN 23.7g; CARB 12.4g; FIBER 2g; CHOL 73mg; IRON 1.2mg; SODIUM 2075mg; CALC 31mg

Prep: 13 min. ✳ **Cook:** 20 min.

Mexican Lime-Chicken Soup

Makes 12 cups

"If I know I have to use chopped vegetables in meals like this one several times during the week, I chop them all at once and then store them in zip-top bags. It's a grind doing it, but it pays off in the long run." —Betsy B., Warrenton, VA

2 Tbsp. vegetable oil
1 large red bell pepper, chopped
1 large onion, chopped
1 tsp. bottled minced garlic
2 (14.5-oz.) cans Mexican-style stewed tomatoes, drained and chopped
2 limes
4 (14-oz.) cans chicken broth

3 cups chopped cooked chicken
¼ cup chopped fresh cilantro
1 Tbsp. chopped fresh or pickled jalapeño pepper
¼ tsp. salt
¼ tsp. pepper
Toppings: shredded Cheddar cheese, sour cream (optional)
Garnish: lime wedges

1. Heat oil in a Dutch oven over medium-high heat. Add bell pepper, onion, and garlic; sauté 3 minutes or until vegetables are tender. Stir in tomatoes, and cook 2 minutes. Cut limes in half crosswise. Squeeze lime juice directly into vegetable mixture; add lime shells and chicken broth to soup. Bring to a boil; reduce heat, and simmer 10 minutes.

2. Remove and discard lime shells. Stir in chicken, cilantro, jalapeño, salt, and pepper. Cook 5 minutes or until thoroughly heated. Serve with toppings and garnish, if desired.

Storage Note: Refrigerate leftovers in an airtight container up to 3 days, or freeze up to 1 month.

Cooking Tip: Simmering the lime shells in the soup imparts a fresh, citrus flavor with virtually no effort.

MENU IDEA FOR 5

- Spicy Black-and-Red Bean Soup
- Cornbread crackers

GROCERIES NEEDED

Check staples: bottled minced garlic, salt

- 1 large onion
- 1 lb. carrots
- 2 (10-oz.) cans chili-style diced tomatoes with green chiles
- 2 (5.5-oz.) cans spicy-hot or regular vegetable juice
- 1 (16-oz.) package frozen shoepeg white corn
- 1 (16-oz.) can kidney beans
- 1 (15-oz.) can black beans
- 1 (14-oz.) can low-sodium beef broth
- 1 box cornbread crackers (such as Town House Bistro Cornbread Crackers)

PER 2 CUPS SOUP: CALORIES 250 (5% from fat); FAT 1.5g (sat 0g, mono 0g, poly 0.1g); PROTEIN 11.4g; CARB 48.8g; FIBER 11.2g; CHOL 0mg; IRON 2.2mg; SODIUM 1398mg; CALC 104mg

Prep: 14 min. ❄ **Cook:** 8 hrs.

Spicy Black-and-Red Bean Soup

Makes 10 cups

For kids and parents watching their weight, this vegetable soup is a great supper choice. It's filling yet low in calories and fat. If you want a mellow flavor, use regular vegetable juice instead of spicy.

1½ cups chopped onion
1¼ cups sliced carrot
2 (10-oz.) cans chili-style diced tomatoes with green chiles
2 (5.5-oz.) cans spicy-hot or regular vegetable juice
1 (16-oz.) package frozen shoepeg white corn, thawed
1 (16-oz.) can kidney beans, drained
1 (15-oz.) can black beans, drained
1 (14-oz.) can low-sodium beef broth
1 tsp. bottled minced garlic
½ tsp. salt

1. Combine all ingredients in a 5-qt. slow cooker. Cover and cook on LOW 8 hours.

Storage Note: Refrigerate leftovers in an airtight container up to 5 days, or freeze up to 1 month.

MENU IDEA FOR 6

- Cheddar-Bacon
  Twice-Baked Potatoes
- Chopped romaine
  salad with tomatoes

GROCERIES NEEDED

Check staples:
vegetable oil, kosher
salt, butter, milk, salt,
pepper, salad dressing

- 6 medium-size baking
  potatoes (about 8 to
  10 oz. each)
- 1 (8-oz.) container
  soft cream cheese
- 1 cup (4 oz.) shred-
  ded sharp Cheddar
  cheese
- 6 fully cooked bacon
  slices
- 1 bunch green onions
- 1 package torn
  romaine lettuce
- 2 tomatoes

PER ENTRÉE SERVING:
CALORIES 471 (57% from fat);
FAT 29.6g (sat 15.2g, mono 5.1g,
poly 3.4g); PROTEIN 12.3g;
CARB 40.1g; FIBER 4.2g;
CHOL 63mg; IRON 2mg;
SODIUM 998mg; CALC 200mg

Prep: 30 min. ❋ **Cook:** 2 hrs. ❋ **Other:** 30 min.

Cheddar-Bacon Twice-Baked Potatoes

Makes 6 servings

Pop these stuffed main-dish potatoes in the oven,
and you're free to help with homework.

6	medium-size baking potatoes
3	Tbsp. vegetable oil
1½	tsp. kosher salt
½	cup soft cream cheese
¼	cup butter or margarine, softened
⅓	cup milk
1	cup (4 oz.) shredded sharp Cheddar cheese
6	fully cooked bacon slices, crumbled
2	green onions, chopped
½	tsp. salt
½	tsp. pepper

1. Preheat oven to 425°. Prick potatoes several times with a fork; place in a large zip-top bag. Add oil and kosher salt; seal and turn bag to coat. Remove potatoes from bag, and place on a baking sheet. Bake at 425° for 1 hour or until tender. Remove from oven, and cool.

2. Cut a 3-inch-wide strip from top of each potato; discard strips. Scoop pulp into a large bowl, leaving shells intact. Mash pulp, cream cheese, butter, and milk with a potato masher; stir in cheese and remaining ingredients. Spoon into shells. Wrap each in aluminum foil; freeze in a large zip-top freezer bag up to 1 month.

3. Preheat oven to 350°. Remove desired number of potatoes from bag; unwrap and discard foil. Bake at 350° for 1 hour or until thoroughly heated.

To serve without freezing: Prepare recipe through Step 2, omitting wrapping and freezing process. Bake at 350° for 35 minutes or until thoroughly heated.

To microwave instead of bake: Microwave 1 potato at MEDIUM HIGH (70% power) for 6 minutes, or microwave 2 potatoes at MEDIUM HIGH for 8 minutes or until hot.

MENU IDEA FOR 8

- Cheese and Tamale Pie
- Guacamole salad

GROCERIES NEEDED

Check staples: salsa, salt, self-rising yellow cornmeal mix, milk, large egg

- 1 lb. ground chuck
- 1 large onion
- 1 large green bell pepper
- 1 (15.5-oz.) can pinto beans
- 1 (14.5-oz.) can diced chili-style or regular tomatoes (such as Del Monte Zesty Chili Style)
- 1 bunch fresh cilantro
- 2 cups (8 oz.) shredded sharp Cheddar cheese
- 2 (8-oz.) packages shredded iceberg lettuce
- 1 (8-oz.) package refrigerated, vacuum-packed prepared guacamole

PER ENTRÉE SERVING:
CALORIES 431(47% from fat); FAT 22.4g (sat 11.2g, mono 5.6g, poly 0.7g); PROTEIN 22.8g; CARB 32.7g; FIBER 5.5g; CHOL 95mg; IRON 3.3mg; SODIUM 988mg; CALC 360mg

Prep: 25 min. ❄ **Cook:** 1 hr., 33 min.

Cheese and Tamale Pie

Makes 8 servings

"My family is all about cheesy, crusty cornbread, so when they saw this emerge from the oven they were all smiles. Considering all I had to do was to pop it in the oven, I was smiling, too."—Kathleen P., Test Kitchens Staff

1   lb. ground chuck
1   large onion, chopped
1   large green bell pepper, chopped
½   cup salsa
1   (15.5-oz.) can pinto beans, drained
1   (14.5-oz.) can diced chili-style or regular tomatoes, drained
½   tsp. salt
½   cup chopped fresh cilantro
2   cups (8 oz.) shredded sharp Cheddar cheese, divided

1⅓   cups self-rising yellow cornmeal mix
1   cup milk
1   large egg, lightly beaten

1. Preheat oven to 400°. Cook first 3 ingredients in a large skillet, stirring until beef crumbles and is no longer pink. Drain and pat dry with paper towels. Return meat mixture to pan; stir in salsa, beans, tomatoes, and salt. Simmer 5 minutes. Stir in cilantro. Spoon mixture into a greased 11- x 7-inch baking dish. Sprinkle with 1 cup cheese.

2. Whisk together cornmeal, milk, and egg in a medium bowl. Stir in remaining 1 cup cheese. Spread batter over beef mixture. Bake at 400° for 20 minutes or until cornbread is lightly browned. Cool completely. Cover tightly with aluminum foil; freeze up to 3 months.

3. Preheat oven to 350°. Remove casserole from freezer; discard foil. Bake at 350° for 1 hour or until thoroughly heated.

To serve without freezing: Prepare recipe through Step 2, omitting covering and freezing procedure.

To thaw and bake: Thaw casserole overnight in refrigerator. Uncover and bake at 350° for 45 minutes or until thoroughly heated.

MENU IDEA FOR 6

- Anytime Chicken and Dressing
- Commercial cranberry-orange relish or cranberry sauce
- Sweet potato fries

GROCERIES NEEDED

Check staples: butter, 2 large eggs, poultry seasoning, vegetable oil

- 1 bunch green onions
- 1 bunch celery
- 10 cornbread muffins
- 1 (16-oz.) package herb-seasoned stuffing mix
- 5 cups chicken broth
- 1½ cups chopped cooked chicken
- Cranberry-orange relish or cranberry sauce
- 3 large sweet potatoes

PER ENTRÉE SERVING:
CALORIES 512 (42% from fat); FAT 24.1g (sat 10.3g, mono 3g, poly 0.8g); PROTEIN 23.5g; CARB 49.8g; FIBER 3.3g; CHOL 175mg; IRON 3.5mg; SODIUM 2311mg; CALC 177mg

Prep: 25 min. ☀ **Cook:** 1 hr., 5 min.

Anytime Chicken and Dressing

Makes 6 servings

"We love this recipe since it's so much like Granny's. Make or purchase cornbread that's to your liking. We prefer cornbread that's not sweet." —Brandi J., Birmingham, AL

¼ cup butter or margarine
7 green onions, chopped
2 celery ribs, chopped

10 cornbread muffins, crumbled (about 3½ cups)
½ (16-oz.) package herb-seasoned stuffing mix
5 cups chicken broth
1½ cups chopped cooked chicken
2 large eggs, lightly beaten
½ tsp. poultry seasoning

1. Melt butter in a large skillet over medium heat; add green onions and celery, and sauté 5 minutes or until tender.

2. Combine cornbread and remaining ingredients in a large bowl; add sautéed vegetable mixture, stirring well. Spoon dressing into a lightly greased 13- x 9-inch baking dish. Cover tightly with heavy-duty aluminum foil; freeze up to 2 months.

3. Preheat oven to 350°. Remove casserole from freezer; remove and discard foil. Bake at 350° for 1 hour or until lightly browned.

To bake without freezing: Prepare recipe through Step 2, omitting covering and freezing process. Bake at 350°, uncovered, for 45 minutes or until lightly browned.

To thaw and bake: Let casserole thaw overnight in refrigerator. Uncover and bake at 350° for 55 minutes or until lightly browned.

Side Dish Note: Sweet potato fries are easy and nutritious. Peel sweet potatoes and cut into ¼-inch strips. Toss with just enough oil to coat, and arrange in a single layer on a baking sheet coated with cooking spray. Bake at 425° for 20 minutes or until edges are lightly browned.

MENU IDEA FOR 6
- Beef Lombardi
- Spring mix salad

GROCERIES NEEDED

Check staples: sugar, salt, pepper, bay leaf, grated Parmesan cheese, salad dressing

- 1 lb. ground chuck
- 1 (14.5-oz.) can diced tomatoes
- 1 (10-oz.) can diced tomatoes and green chiles
- 1 (6-oz.) can tomato paste
- 1 (8-oz.) package medium egg noodles
- 1 bunch green onions
- 1 (8-oz.) container sour cream
- 1 cup (4 oz.) shredded sharp Cheddar cheese
- 1 cup (4 oz.) shredded mozzarella cheese
- 2 (10-oz.) packages spring mix (such as Fresh Express)

PER ENTRÉE SERVING:
CALORIES 642 (55% from fat); FAT 38.9g (sat 19.8g, mono 10.6g, poly 1.4g); PROTEIN 34.8g; CARB 40.2g; FIBER 4.8g; CHOL 136mg; IRON 3.9mg; SODIUM 1540mg; CALC 516mg

Prep: 20 min. ✳ **Cook:** 1 hr., 2 min.

Beef Lombardi

Makes 6 servings

This recipe offers the same robust Italian flavors and cheesy filling as a stuffed manicotti with a fraction of the hassle. Amy H. of Lafayette, CO, points out how nice it is that only 1 ingredient needs to be chopped.

1 lb. ground chuck
1 (14.5-oz.) can diced tomatoes, undrained
1 (10-oz.) can diced tomatoes and green chiles, undrained
2 tsp. sugar
1½ tsp. salt
¼ tsp. pepper
1 (6-oz.) can tomato paste
1 bay leaf

1 (8-oz.) package medium egg noodles
6 green onions, chopped
1 (8-oz.) container sour cream
1 cup (4 oz.) shredded sharp Cheddar cheese
1 cup grated Parmesan cheese
1 cup (4 oz.) shredded mozzarella cheese

Garnish: freshly ground pepper

1. Cook beef in a large skillet over medium heat, stirring until it crumbles and is no longer pink. Drain well, and pat dry with paper towels. Wipe skillet clean, and return meat to pan. Stir in diced tomatoes and next 4 ingredients; cook 5 minutes. Add tomato paste and bay leaf, and simmer 30 minutes, stirring occasionally.

2. Meanwhile, cook egg noodles according to package directions; drain and return to pan. Stir in green onions and sour cream. Spoon noodle mixture in a lightly greased 13- x 9-inch baking dish. Top with beef mixture; sprinkle with cheeses. Cover tightly with aluminum foil, and freeze up to 1 month.

3. Remove casserole from freezer, and thaw overnight in refrigerator.

4. Preheat oven to 350°. Bake, covered with aluminum foil, at 350° for 35 minutes. Uncover casserole, and bake 5 more minutes. Garnish, if desired.

To bake without freezing: Prepare recipe through Step 2, omitting the covering and freezing process. Bake at 350°, uncovered, for 35 minutes.

MENU IDEA FOR 8

- Smoked Turkey Tetrazzini

- French bread

GROCERIES NEEDED

Check staples: butter, bottled minced garlic, grated Parmesan cheese, salt, pepper

- 12 oz. vermicelli or thin spaghetti

- 1 medium onion

- 1 (8-oz.) package sliced fresh mushrooms

- 1½ lb. smoked or honey-roasted turkey

- 1¼ cups (6 oz.) shredded Cheddar cheese

- 1 (10¾-oz.) can cream of mushroom soup

- 1 (10¾-oz.) can cream of celery soup

- 1 (8-oz.) container sour cream

- 1 (14-oz.) can chicken broth

- 1 loaf French bread

PER ENTRÉE SERVING:
CALORIES 499 (38% from fat); FAT 21.1g (sat 10.6g, mono 4.4g, poly 1.1g); PROTEIN 34.8g; CARB 41.8g; FIBER 2.5g; CHOL 89mg; IRON 2.7mg; SODIUM 1222mg; CALC 220mg

Prep: 25 min. ※ **Cook:** 2 hrs., 25 min.

Smoked Turkey Tetrazzini

Makes 8 servings

"I like to have something in the freezer so on the spur of the moment I can take a meal to a family in need. This recipe is perfect for that since it makes 2 casseroles."—Sonya L., Ridgeland, MS

12 oz. vermicelli, broken in half
1 Tbsp. butter or margarine
1 medium onion, chopped
1 (8-oz) package sliced fresh mushrooms
1 tsp. bottled minced garlic
4 cups cubed smoked or honey-roasted turkey (about 1½ lb.)
1¼ cups (6 oz.) shredded Cheddar cheese, divided
¼ cup grated Parmesan cheese
1 (10¾-oz.) can cream of mushroom soup
1 (10¾-oz.) can cream of celery soup
1 (8-oz.) container sour cream
½ cup chicken broth
½ tsp. salt
½ tsp. pepper

1. Preheat oven to 350°. Cook vermicelli according to package directions. Meanwhile, melt butter in a Dutch oven over medium-high heat; add onion, mushrooms, and garlic; sauté 5 minutes or until tender. Stir in turkey, ¾ cup Cheddar cheese, and remaining 7 ingredients. Drain vermicelli, and add to turkey mixture; stir well.

2. Spoon mixture into 2 lightly greased 8-inch square baking dishes; sprinkle with remaining Cheddar cheese. Cover each casserole tightly in aluminum foil; freeze up to 2 months.

3. Preheat oven to 350°. Remove desired number of casseroles from freezer, leaving foil cover intact. Bake at 350° for 2 hours; uncover and bake 15 minutes or until bubbly.

To bake without freezing: Prepare recipe through Step 2, omitting the covering and freezing process. Bake, uncovered, at 350° for 30 minutes or until bubbly.

To thaw and bake: Let desired number of casseroles thaw overnight in refrigerator. Leave foil cover intact, and bake at 350° for 1 hour, 15 minutes. Uncover and bake 15 more minutes or until bubbly.

MENU IDEA FOR 8

- Taco Casserole
- Bananas sprinkled with lime juice and brown sugar

GROCERIES NEEDED

Check staples: bottled minced garlic, pepper, brown sugar

- 2 lb. ground chuck
- 1 large onion
- 1 (15-oz.) can ranch-style beans
- 1 (10³/₄-oz.) can cream of chicken soup
- 1 (10³/₄-oz.) can cream of mushroom soup
- 1 (10-oz.) can diced tomatoes and green chiles
- 8 (6-inch) white corn tortillas
- 1 (8-oz.) package pasteurized prepared cheese product crumbles (such as Velveeta Crumbles)
- 1 bunch fresh cilantro (optional)
- 4 bananas
- 1 lime

PER ENTRÉE SERVING:
CALORIES 574 (55% from fat);
FAT 35.2g (sat 14.3g, mono 12.2g,
poly 1.4g); PROTEIN 30.9g;
CARB 32.8g; FIBER 4.9g;
CHOL 103mg; IRON 4mg;
SODIUM 1642mg; CALC 257mg

Prep: 15 min. ※ **Cook:** 1 hr., 35 min. ※ **Other:** 10 min.

Taco Casserole

Makes 8 servings

To prepare this recipe in individual portions, assemble in 8 (16-oz.) microwave-safe containers. Cover them tightly in foil, and freeze up to 1 month. To cook one at a time, remove and discard the foil, and microwave at 70% power for 4 minutes or until hot.

2 lb. ground chuck
1 large onion, chopped
1 tsp. bottled minced garlic
½ tsp. pepper
1 (15-oz.) can ranch-style beans
1 (10³/₄-oz.) can cream of chicken soup
1 (10³/₄-oz.) can cream of mushroom soup
1 (10-oz.) can diced tomatoes and green chiles, undrained

8 (6-inch) white corn tortillas, cut into quarters
1 (8-oz.) package pasteurized prepared cheese product crumbles
Garnish: fresh cilantro sprigs

1. Cook first 4 ingredients in a large skillet, stirring until beef crumbles and is no longer pink. Drain; pat dry with paper towels. Wipe skillet clean. Return meat mixture to pan; stir in beans and next 3 ingredients.

2. Layer half of tortillas in a lightly greased 13- x 9-inch baking dish. Top with half of meat mixture and half of cheese crumbles. Repeat layers with remaining tortilla wedges, meat mixture, and cheese crumbles. Cover tightly with aluminum foil; freeze up to 1 month.

3. Preheat oven to 350°. Remove casserole from freezer. Bake, covered, at 350° for 1 hour. Remove and discard foil. Bake 30 more minutes or until thoroughly heated. Let stand 10 minutes before serving. Garnish, if desired.

To bake without freezing: Prepare recipe through Step 2, omitting covering and freezing process. Bake at 350°, uncovered, for 30 minutes or until thoroughly heated.

To thaw and bake: Let casserole thaw overnight in refrigerator. Bake, uncovered, at 350° for 1 hour or until thoroughly heated.

MENU IDEA FOR 8

- Warm Ham and Cheese Croissandwiches
- Seedless green grapes and pineapple chunks

GROCERIES NEEDED:

Check staples: butter, mayonnaise, coarse-grained mustard, poppy seeds (optional)

- 1 small onion
- 8 large croissants
- 1 lb. deli ham, thinly sliced
- 8 (1-oz.) Swiss cheese slices
- 1 lb. seedless green grapes
- 1 cored fresh pineapple

PER ENTRÉE SERVING:
CALORIES 512 (58% from fat); FAT 32.8g (sat 16.6g, mono 6.7g, poly 1.3g); PROTEIN 22.3g; CARB 29.6g; FIBER 2.3g; CHOL 107mg; IRON 1.8mg; SODIUM 1083mg; CALC 313mg

Prep: 25 min. ❊ **Cook:** 1 hr.

Warm Ham and Cheese Croissandwiches

Makes 8 sandwiches

After tossing these sandwiches in the oven, you'll have ample time to listen to phone messages and review schoolwork.

¼ cup butter or margarine, softened
¼ cup mayonnaise
3 Tbsp. coarse-grained mustard
1 Tbsp. grated onion
2 tsp. poppy seeds (optional)
8 large croissants, split in half
1 lb. deli ham, thinly sliced
8 (1-oz.) Swiss cheese slices, cut in half

1. Stir together first 5 ingredients in a small bowl. Spread evenly over cut sides of croissants. Top bottom halves evenly with ham and cheese; top with remaining croissant halves. Wrap each sandwich in aluminum foil, and place in large zip-top freezer bags. Freeze up to 1 month.

2. Preheat oven to 350°. Remove desired number of sandwiches from plastic bags and place on a baking sheet. (Do not remove foil.) Bake at 350° for 1 hour or until thoroughly heated.

To bake without freezing: Prepare recipe through Step 1, omitting wrapping and freezing process. Place sandwiches on a baking sheet, and bake at 350° for 13 to 15 minutes or until thoroughly heated.

To microwave frozen sandwiches: Remove and discard aluminum foil from desired number of sandwiches. Microwave 1 sandwich at a time at MEDIUM (50% power) for 2 minutes or until thoroughly heated.

Crunchy Ranch Tortilla Chicken

Makes 8 servings

"Although I know I should, I don't typically involve my boys in meal preparation. But this recipe is so easy I decided to give it a try. I got them to roll up their sleeves and get into it. We all loved it!" —Carrie D., San Clemente, CA

1 (1-oz.) envelope Ranch-style dressing mix, divided
2 lb. chicken tenders

¾ cup buttermilk
1 large egg
½ cup all-purpose flour
1 (13-oz.) package Ranch-flavored tortilla chips, finely crushed
Vegetable cooking spray

1. Preheat oven to 450°. Sprinkle 1 Tbsp. dressing mix evenly over chicken.

2. Whisk together buttermilk, egg, and remaining dressing mix. Place flour and crushed tortilla chips in separate shallow dishes. Dredge chicken tenders in flour; dip in buttermilk mixture, and roll in crushed chips. Coat chicken lightly on all sides with cooking spray. Set aside.

3. Place a large baking sheet in 450° oven for 5 minutes. Place chicken on hot pan. Bake 18 minutes or until crust is lightly browned. Cool completely. Place chicken in a large zip-top freezer bag. Seal and freeze up to 1 month.

4. Preheat oven to 425°. Remove desired amount of chicken from plastic bag, and place on a baking sheet. Bake at 425° for 20 minutes or until hot and crisp.

To serve without freezing: Prepare recipe through Step 3, omitting the wrapping, sealing, and freezing process.

MENU IDEA FOR 8
- Crunchy Ranch Tortilla Chicken
- Fresh carrot and celery sticks with Ranch dressing

GROCERIES NEEDED

Check staples: large egg, all-purpose flour, vegetable cooking spray
- 1 (1-oz.) envelope Ranch-style dressing mix
- 2 lb. chicken tenders
- 1 small carton buttermilk
- 1 (13-oz.) package Ranch-flavored tortilla chips
- 1 lb. fresh carrots
- 1 bunch celery
- 1 bottle Ranch dressing

PER ENTRÉE SERVING:
CALORIES 411 (30% from fat); FAT 13.8g (sat 3.2g, mono 7.1g, poly 2g); PROTEIN 32g; CARB 38.7g; FIBER 2g; CHOL 96mg; IRON 2mg; SODIUM 640mg; CALC 82mg

Prep: 25 min. ❈ Cook: 1 hr. ❈ Other: 1 hr., 10 min.

Spicy-Sweet Meat Loaves

Makes 8 servings

Placing the unwrapped loaves in the freezer for 1 hour in step 2 allows them to partially freeze so they'll be easier to wrap in foil. In case you get sidetracked, set a timer as a reminder to finish wrapping them.

3 lb. ground chuck
2 large eggs, lightly beaten
1 small green bell pepper, finely chopped
1 small onion, finely chopped
1 cup fine, dry breadcrumbs
¾ cup finely chopped smoked ham
⅓ cup ketchup
2 Tbsp. brown sugar
1 Tbsp. hot sauce
1½ cups tomato sauce, divided

8 bacon slices

1. Combine first 9 ingredients in a large bowl; stir in 1 cup tomato sauce.

2. Shape mixture into 2 (9- x 4-inch) loaves. Place on a baking sheet, and freeze 1 hour. Wrap loaves tightly in aluminum foil, and freeze up to 1 month.

3. Remove meat loaves from freezer, and thaw overnight in refrigerator.

4. Preheat oven to 350°. Remove and discard aluminum foil; place meat loaves on a broiler pan. Pour remaining ½ cup tomato sauce over meat loaves. Arrange 4 bacon slices over each loaf. Bake at 350° for 1 hour. Let stand 10 minutes before serving.

To bake without freezing: Prepare recipe through shaping procedure in Step 2. Proceed with recipe in Step 4, omitting unwrapping procedure.

Mini Spicy-Sweet Meat Loaves: Shape mixture into 8 (4- x 3-inch) loaves. Wrap and freeze as directed. Thaw meat loaves overnight in refrigerator. Unwrap and brush each loaf with 1 Tbsp. tomato sauce. Arrange 2 halved bacon slices over each loaf. Bake at 350° for 40 to 45 minutes.

MENU IDEA FOR 8

- Spicy-Sweet Meat Loaves
- Mashed potatoes with skins
- Steamed green beans

GROCERIES NEEDED

Check staples: large eggs; fine, dry breadcrumbs; ketchup; brown sugar; hot sauce

- 3 lb. ground chuck
- 1 small green bell pepper
- 1 small onion
- ¾ cup finely chopped smoked ham
- 1 (15-oz.) can tomato sauce
- 8 bacon slices
- 2 (24-oz.) packages refrigerated mashed potatoes with skins
- 2 lb. fresh green beans or 2 (16-oz.) packages frozen green beans

PER ENTRÉE SERVING:
CALORIES 594 (59% from fat); FAT 39.1g (sat 14.6g, mono 16.9g, poly 1.7g); PROTEIN 38.1g; CARB 20.2g; FIBER 1.3g; CHOL 186mg; IRON 4.8mg; SODIUM 871mg; CALC 71mg

MENU IDEA FOR 6

- Southwest Corn and Sausage Dressing
- Avocado wedges with shredded lettuce, salsa, and sour cream

GROCERIES NEEDED

Check staples: butter, large eggs, salsa

- 1 lb. ground pork sausage
- 1 medium onion
- 1 (8.5-oz.) package corn muffin mix (we tested with Jiffy)
- 1 (14³/₄-oz.) can cream-style corn
- 1 (15-oz.) can black beans
- 1 (4.5-oz.) can chopped green chiles
- 2 cups (8 oz.) shredded Cheddar cheese
- 2 large avocados
- 1 (8-oz.) package shredded iceberg lettuce
- 1 (8-oz.) container sour cream

PER ENTRÉE SERVING:
CALORIES 809 (60% from fat); FAT 54.3g (sat 26.3g, mono 17.1g, poly 4g); PROTEIN 29g; CARB 52.8g; FIBER 4.6g; CHOL 205mg; IRON 3.4mg; SODIUM 1520mg; CALC 315mg

Prep: 10 min. ❄ **Cook:** 2 hrs., 5 min.

Southwest Corn and Sausage Dressing

Makes 6 servings

Similar to Southern cornbread dressing, this one-dish casserole can be made spicier by using hot sausage. Alicia K. from Walhalla, SC, loved it because it could be frozen in advance for covered-dish suppers.

1 lb. ground pork sausage
1 medium onion, chopped

1 (8.5-oz.) package corn muffin mix
1 (14³/₄-oz.) can cream-style corn
½ cup butter or margarine, melted
2 large eggs
1 (15-oz.) can black beans, drained and rinsed
1 (4.5-oz.) can chopped green chiles, drained
2 cups (8 oz.) shredded Cheddar cheese

1. Cook sausage and onion in a large skillet over medium-high heat, stirring until sausage crumbles and is no longer pink. Drain well.

2. Combine corn muffin mix and next 3 ingredients in a large bowl. Stir in cooked sausage mixture, black beans, green chiles, and cheese. Spoon cornbread mixture into a lightly greased 11- x 7-inch baking dish. Cover tightly with aluminum foil; freeze up to 1 month.

3. Preheat oven to 350°. Remove dressing from freezer. Bake, covered, at 350° for 1 hour. Remove and discard foil; bake 1 more hour or until golden brown and set.

To bake without freezing: Prepare recipe through Step 2, omitting the covering and freezing process. Bake at 350°, uncovered, for 1 hour or until golden brown and set.

To thaw and bake: Let dressing thaw overnight in refrigerator. Bake, covered, 30 minutes. Remove and discard foil. Bake 1 more hour.

MENU IDEA FOR 4

- Chili-Lime Grouper Fillets
- Mexicorn
- Kiwifruit

GROCERIES NEEDED

Check staples: vegetable oil, chili powder, salt, garlic powder

- 3 limes
- 1 small carton orange juice
- 1 bunch green onions
- 8 (6-oz.) grouper fillets
- 2 (12-oz.) cans Mexicorn
- 4 kiwifruit

PER ENTRÉE SERVING:
CALORIES 177 (18% from fat);
FAT 3.5g (sat 0.6g, mono 1.1g,
poly 1.3g); PROTEIN 33.1g;
CARB 1.5g; FIBER 0.2g;
CHOL 63mg; IRON 1.6mg;
SODIUM 174mg; CALC 51mg

Prep: 7 min. ❋ **Cook:** 10 min. ❋ **Other:** 30 min.

Chili-Lime Grouper Fillets

Makes 8 servings (save 4 fillets for recipe on following pages)

"These fillets were a super hit! The best part of this recipe is knowing I have a headstart for another meal I'm certain my family will enjoy." —Annemarie H., Woodstock, IL

2 Tbsp. fresh lime juice
2 Tbsp. orange juice
2 Tbsp. vegetable oil
4 green onions, chopped
2 tsp. chili powder
½ tsp. salt
½ tsp. garlic powder

8 (6-oz.) grouper fillets

2 limes, each cut into 4 wedges

1. Combine first 7 ingredients in a large zip-top freezer bag.

2. Add fish to bag; seal bag, and marinate in refrigerator 30 minutes, turning bag once.

3. Preheat grill to medium-high (350° to 400°).

4. Remove fish from marinade, discarding marinade. Grill fish, uncovered, over medium-high heat 5 minutes on each side or until fish flakes with a fork. Transfer fish to a serving platter, and drizzle with fresh lime juice.

Note about Planned-Overs: Cover and refrigerate 4 Chili-Lime Grouper Fillets to prepare Fish Tacos (following pages) up to 2 days later, if desired.

MENU IDEA FOR 4

- Fish Tacos
- Deli carrot-raisin salad

GROCERIES NEEDED

Planned-overs needed: 4 Chili-Lime Grouper Fillets

- 1 (8-oz.) container sour cream
- 1 bunch fresh cilantro
- 1 lime
- 1 bunch green onions
- 8 (6-inch) corn tortillas
- 1 large tomato
- 1 cup (4 oz.) shredded Cheddar cheese
- 1 small package shredded iceberg lettuce
- 1 pt. deli carrot-raisin salad

PER ENTRÉE SERVING:
CALORIES 384 (36% from fat);
FAT 15.3g (sat 7.3g, mono 4.2g, poly 2.2g); PROTEIN 40g;
CARB 23.1g; FIBER 02.7g;
CHOL 90mg; IRON 1.9mg;
SODIUM 291mg; CALC 216mg

Prep: 10 min. ❄ **Cook:** 5 min.

Fish Tacos

Makes 4 servings

"My family laps up these tacos faster than ordinary beef or chicken tacos. The only thing I do differently is add a teaspoon or two of minced jalapeño pepper to the sour cream sauce. We love it with the kick!"—Kelly W., Food Stylist

½ cup sour cream
¼ cup chopped fresh cilantro
2 Tbsp. fresh lime juice
2 green onions, chopped

4 Chili-Lime Grouper Fillets (previous pages)

8 (6-inch) corn tortillas
Toppings: chopped tomato, shredded Cheddar cheese, shredded iceberg lettuce

1. Combine first 4 ingredients in a small bowl, stirring well to combine. Set sauce aside.

2. Place fish in a microwave-safe bowl, and cover with plastic wrap. Microwave at MEDIUM-HIGH (70% power) for 3 minutes or until fish is hot. Flake fish into bite-size pieces with a fork.

3. Heat tortillas according to package directions. Divide fish evenly over tortillas, and top with desired toppings. Serve with sauce, and fold in half.

MENU IDEA FOR 6

- Brown-Sugared Pork Tenderloin
- Grilled corn on the cob and green onions
- Tomato wedges

GROCERIES NEEDED

Check staples: cider vinegar, light brown sugar, salt, bottled minced garlic, paprika, dried crushed red pepper

- 2 (2-lb.) packages pork tenderloin
- 6 ears corn
- 1 bunch green onions
- 3 tomatoes

PER ENTRÉE SERVING:
CALORIES 227 (33% from fat);
FAT 8.3g (sat 2.8g, mono 3.7g,
poly 0.9g); PROTEIN 31.1g;
CARB 4.7g; FIBER 0.1g;
CHOL 100mg; IRON 2mg;
SODIUM 270mg; CALC 13mg

Prep: 5 min. ❈ **Cook:** 24 min. ❈ **Other:** 40 min.

Brown-Sugared Pork Tenderloin

Makes 12 servings (save half for recipe on following pages)

It's not crucial to use a meat thermometer for this recipe. Instead, visually check for doneness. Cut into the thickest portion of the tenderloin with a sharp knife. When cooked properly, pork should be slightly pink in the center and the juices clear.

½ cup cider vinegar
¼ cup firmly packed light brown sugar
1 tsp. salt
1 tsp. bottled minced garlic
½ tsp. paprika
½ tsp. dried crushed red pepper

2 (2-lb.) packages pork tenderloin

1. Combine first 6 ingredients in a large zip-top freezer bag. Add pork to bag; seal bag, and marinate in refrigerator 30 minutes, turning bag once.

2. Preheat grill to medium-high (350° to 400°). Drain marinade from plastic bag into a small saucepan; bring to a boil. Boil 1 minute. Remove from heat, and set aside.

3. Grill tenderloins, uncovered, over medium-high heat 10 to 12 minutes on each side or until pork is barely pink inside or a meat thermometer inserted in thickest portion of tenderloin registers 155°, basting often with reserved marinade. Remove from grill; let stand 10 minutes or until temperature reaches 160°.

Note about Planned-Overs: Cover and refrigerate 2 Brown-Sugared Pork Tenderloins to prepare Pork Fajitas (following pages) up to 3 days later, if desired.

MENU IDEA FOR 6

- Pork Fajitas

- Yellow rice with cilantro

GROCERIES NEEDED

Check staples: vegetable oil, salsa

Planned-overs needed: 2 Brown-Sugared Pork Tenderloins

- 1 red bell pepper

- 1 green bell pepper

- 1 medium onion

- Fajita seasoning (we tested with McCormick)

- 12 (8-inch) flour tortillas

- 1 (8-oz.) package shredded Cheddar cheese

- 1 (8-oz.) package refrigerated, vacuum-packed prepared guacamole

- 1 (8-oz.) container sour cream

- 1 (10-oz.) package yellow rice (such as Vigo)

- 1 bunch cilantro

PER ENTRÉE SERVING:
CALORIES 684 (36% from fat);
FAT 27.2g (sat 9.1g, mono 9.9g,
poly 3.2g); PROTEIN 43.7g;
CARB 64.7g; FIBER 2.6g;
CHOL 120mg; IRON 4.4mg;
SODIUM 1543mg; CALC 308mg

Prep: 10 min. ❊ **Cook:** 10 min. ❊ **Other:** 10 min.

Pork Fajitas

Makes 6 servings

Check the produce section of your grocery store for fresh, precut bell peppers and onions to save prep time.

2 Brown-Sugared Pork Tenderloins (previous pages)
1 red bell pepper, cut into strips
1 green bell pepper, cut into strips
1 medium onion, cut in half and vertically sliced
2 Tbsp. fajita seasoning
1 Tbsp. vegetable oil

12 (8-inch) flour tortillas

Toppings: shredded Cheddar cheese, guacamole, sour cream, salsa

1. Cut pork tenderloins in half lengthwise. Place cut side down, and cut into ¼-inch slices. Combine pork and next 3 ingredients in a large bowl. Sprinkle with fajita seasoning, tossing gently. Let stand 10 minutes.

2. Heat oil in a large skillet over medium-high heat. Add pork mixture; sauté 4 minutes or just until vegetables are crisp-tender.

3. Heat tortillas according to package directions. Serve pork mixture immediately in warm tortillas with toppings.

144

MENU IDEA FOR 4

- French Onion Pot Roast
- Whole fresh fruit

GROCERIES NEEDED

Check staples: salt, pepper, bay leaf

- Slow cooker liners (we tested with Reynolds)
- 6 small red potatoes
- 4 medium carrots
- 1 large onion
- 1 (4- to 4½-lb.) chuck roast
- 1 (10¾-oz.) can condensed French onion soup
- 1 (10¾-oz.) can golden mushroom soup
- 1 bunch fresh rosemary (optional)
- Whole fresh fruit

PER ENTRÉE SERVING:
CALORIES 520 (38% from fat); FAT 22.2g (sat 7.6g, mono 8.4g, poly 1.1g); PROTEIN 47.1g; CARB 30.2g; FIBER 3.7g; CHOL 142mg; IRON 6mg; SODIUM 809mg; CALC 44mg

Prep: 10 min. ✳ **Cook:** 8 hrs.

French Onion Pot Roast

Makes 8 servings (save 3 cups beef and 1½ cups cooking juices for recipe on following pages)

This recipe comes together quickly with virtually no mess. Begin by lining the slow cooker with a disposable slow cooker liner, and cleanup at the end of the day will be just as effortless.

6 small red potatoes, cut in half
4 medium carrots, cut into 1-inch pieces
1 large onion, cut into 6 wedges
1 (4- to 4½-lb.) chuck roast, trimmed and cut in half
¼ tsp. salt
½ tsp. pepper

1 (10¾-oz.) can condensed French onion soup
1 (10¾-oz.) can golden mushroom soup
½ cup water
1 bay leaf
Fresh rosemary sprig (optional)

1. Place first 3 ingredients in a 5- to 6-qt. slow cooker. Place roast on vegetables, and sprinkle with salt and pepper.

2. Whisk together French onion soup, mushroom soup, and water; pour mixture evenly over beef. Add bay leaf. Cover and cook on HIGH 1 hour. Reduce heat to LOW, and cook 7 hours or until tender.

3. Remove roast and vegetables from slow cooker; keep warm. Skim fat from cooking juices. Serve cooking juices with roast and vegetables. Garnish, if desired.

Note about Planned-Overs: Cover and refrigerate 3 cups beef and 1½ cups cooking juices from French Onion Pot Roast to prepare French Dip Sandwiches (following pages) up to 3 days later, if desired.

146

Prep: 8 min. ❄ **Cook:** 4 min.

French Dip Sandwiches

Makes 4 servings

"My boys are ravenous when they come home after a long, hard football practice. Fortunately this recipe comes together quick and is hearty enough to satisfy. I encourage them to eat fresh fruit while I assemble the sandwiches." —Susan C., Memphis, TN

MENU IDEA FOR 4

- French Dip Sandwiches
- Steak fries
- Seedless red grapes

GROCERIES NEEDED

Planned-overs needed: 3 cups beef from French Onion Pot Roast and 1¹/₂ cups cooking juices

- 4 (6-inch) hoagie rolls
- ¹/₄ cup prepared horseradish sauce (such as Heinz)
- 1 (8-oz.) package provolone cheese slices
- 1 large bag frozen steak fries
- 1 lb. seedless red grapes

PER ENTRÉE SERVING:
CALORIES 784 (45% from fat); FAT 39.1g (sat 17.1g, mono 12g, poly 1.1g); PROTEIN 62.1g; CARB 45.9g; FIBER 2.3g; CHOL 157mg; IRON 7.8mg; SODIUM 1744mg; CALC 507mg

4   (6-inch) hoagie rolls, split
¹/₄ cup prepared horseradish sauce or mayonnaise

3   cups beef from French Onion Pot Roast (previous pages), shredded
1¹/₂ cups cooking juices from French Onion Pot Roast (previous pages)
1   (8-oz.) package provolone cheese slices (8 slices)

1. Preheat broiler.

2. Spread bottom half of each hoagie roll with horseradish sauce, and place on a baking sheet.

3. Combine shredded roast and cooking juices in a microwave-safe bowl. Cover and cook at HIGH 3 minutes or until thoroughly heated, stirring once. Remove roast with a slotted spoon and divide evenly on bottom halves of rolls; top each with 2 slices cheese.

4. Broil about 5 inches from heat 1 minute or until cheese melts. Cover with top halves of rolls, and serve with reserved juices for dipping.

MENU IDEA FOR 4

- Hoisin-Marinated Pork Chops
- Couscous
- Cooked carrots

GROCERIES NEEDED

Check staples: hoisin sauce, teriyaki sauce, rice vinegar, soy sauce, honey, bottled minced garlic, ground ginger

- 8 (¹/₂-inch) bone-in pork loin chops (about 8 oz. each)
- 1 (10-oz.) box couscous
- 1 lb. carrots

PER ENTRÉE SERVING:
CALORIES 350 (48% from fat); FAT 18.5g (sat 6.9g, mono 8.1g, poly 1.7g); PROTEIN 37g; CARB 6.4g; FIBER 0.2g; CHOL 111mg; IRON 1.5mg; SODIUM 553mg; CALC 37mg

Prep: 5 min. ❋ **Cook:** 16 min. ❋ **Other:** 30 min.

Hoisin-Marinated Pork Chops

Makes 8 servings (save 4 pork chops for recipe on following pages)

This marinade is concentrated so it penetrates the chops in a short amount of time.

¼ cup hoisin sauce
¼ cup teriyaki sauce
2 Tbsp. rice vinegar
2 Tbsp. soy sauce
2 Tbsp. honey
1 tsp. bottled minced garlic
½ tsp. ground ginger

8 (¹/₂-inch) bone-in pork loin chops (about 8 oz. each)

1. Whisk together first 7 ingredients in a glass measuring cup. Pour ½ cup hoisin mixture into a large zip-top freezer bag. Reserve remaining ¼ cup hoisin mixture.

2. Add pork chops to bag; seal bag, and marinate in refrigerator no longer than 30 minutes, turning bag once.

3. Preheat grill to medium-high (350° to 400°).

4. Remove pork from bag; discard marinade. Grill chops, covered, over medium-high heat 7 to 8 minutes on each side or until done, basting with reserved marinade during the last 5 minutes.

Note about Planned-Overs: Cover and refrigerate 4 Hoisin-Marinated Pork Chops to prepare Pork Lettuce Wraps (following pages), if desired.

Prep: 12 min. ❋ **Cook:** 5 min.

Pork Lettuce Wraps

Makes 6 servings

"My family loves Chinese food, and this is better than what you get at a restaurant. The aroma makes the house smell great."—Kimberly M., Laguna Niguel, CA

4 Hoisin-Marinated Pork Chops
(previous pages)
2 tsp. vegetable oil
1 Tbsp. bottled minced ginger

2 Tbsp. rice wine vinegar
2 Tbsp. teriyaki sauce
2 Tbsp. soy sauce
2 Tbsp. honey
1 Tbsp. chili-garlic sauce
1 tsp. cornstarch
2 cups shredded carrots
3 green onions, thinly sliced
½ cup dry-roasted peanuts, chopped

1 head iceberg lettuce, cut in half and
separated into leaves (see tip)
Bottled peanut sauce (optional)
Soy sauce (optional)

1. Remove pork from bones; cut pork into ½-inch pieces. Heat oil in a large skillet over medium-high heat. Add pork and ginger; sauté 2 minutes.

2. Whisk together vinegar and next 5 ingredients in a small bowl. Add vinegar mixture, carrots, and green onions to pork. Cook 3 minutes or until mixture thickens slightly, stirring often. Stir in peanuts.

3. Spoon mixture onto lettuce leaves; roll up. Serve with peanut sauce and additional soy sauce, if desired.

Serving tip: To separate iceberg lettuce leaves easily and without tearing, cut the head in half first (cutting through stem end). Boston lettuce has a buttery texture and is a great alternative.

MENU IDEA FOR 6

* Pork Lettuce Wraps
* Pineapple sorbet

GROCERIES NEEDED

Check staples: vegetable oil, bottled minced ginger, rice wine vinegar, teriyaki sauce, soy sauce, honey, cornstarch

Planned-overs needed: 4 Hoisin Marinated Pork Chops

* 1 Tbsp. chili-garlic sauce (we tested with Lee Kum Kee)
* 2 cups shredded carrots
* 1 bunch green onions
* ½ cup dry-roasted peanuts, chopped
* 1 head iceberg lettuce
* Bottled peanut sauce (we tested with House of Tsang)
* ½ gallon pineapple sorbet

PER ENTRÉE SERVING:
CALORIES 382 (47% from fat); FAT 20.1g (sat 5.6g, mono 9g, poly 3.8g); PROTEIN 29.9g; CARB 21.3g; FIBER 3.4g; CHOL 74mg; IRON 2mg; SODIUM 1089mg; CALC 67mg

GROCERIES NEEDED

Check staples:
ketchup, butter, light brown sugar, cider vinegar, Worcestershire sauce, prepared mustard, salt, pepper, bottled barbecue sauce

- 8 (10-oz.) bone-in chicken breasts
- 1 medium onion
- 1 package sandwich buns
- 1 small jar pickle slices
- 1 (32-oz.) bag frozen French fries

PER ENTRÉE SERVING:
CALORIES 321 (24% from fat); FAT 8.4g (sat 4.3g, mono 2.1g, poly 0.9g); PROTEIN 43.3g; CARB 16.7g; FIBER 0.3g; CHOL 122mg; IRON 1.9mg; SODIUM 688mg; CALC 42mg

Prep: 7 min. ❋ **Cook:** 8 hrs.

Easy Barbecued Chicken

Makes 8 servings (save 3 cups for recipe on following pages)

"This chicken is so fall-apart tender, it takes only a moment to bone and shred. You'll agree it's simple and versatile, too. My family likes it served in buns with barbecue sauce. I prefer it piled high on a baked potato." —Karen S., Indian Springs, AL

8 (10-oz.) bone-in chicken breasts, skinned
1 medium onion, chopped

1 cup ketchup
¼ cup butter or margarine, melted
¼ cup firmly packed light brown sugar
2 Tbsp. cider vinegar
2 Tbsp. Worcestershire sauce
1 Tbsp. prepared mustard
½ tsp. salt
¼ tsp. pepper

1. Place chicken in a 5-qt. slow cooker; top with onion.

2. Whisk together ketchup and remaining ingredients; pour over chicken and onions. Cover and cook on HIGH 1 hour. Reduce heat to LOW, and cook 7 hours. Remove chicken from sauce; cool.

3. Remove chicken from bones, discarding bones. Shred chicken, and stir into sauce.

Note about Planned-Overs: Cover and refrigerate 3 cups Easy Barbecued Chicken to prepare Hearty Brunswick Stew (following pages) up to 3 days later, if desired.

MENU IDEA FOR 6

- Hearty Brunswick Stew
- Corn muffins
- Red plums

GROCERIES NEEDED

Check staples: salt, pepper

Planned-overs needed: 3 cups Easy Barbecued Chicken

- 2 (14-oz.) cans chicken broth
- 1 (1-lb.) package frozen corn kernels
- 1 (10-oz.) package frozen baby lima beans
- 1 (20-oz.) package refrigerated diced potatoes with onions
- 1 (8-oz.) can tomato sauce
- 6 deli corn muffins
- 6 red plums

PER 1¹/₂ CUPS STEW:
CALORIES 319 (16% from fat);
FAT 5.8g (sat 2.2g, mono 1.2g, poly 0.7g); PROTEIN 27.9g;
CARB 39.1g; FIBER 4.5g;
CHOL 67mg; IRON 2.3mg;
SODIUM 1614mg; CALC 33mg

Prep: 5 min. ❋ **Cook:** 25 min.

Hearty Brunswick Stew

Makes 9 cups

This stew has long-simmered flavor but is made in record time. Cindy Lee from Mt. Airy, MD, gave it her family's seal of approval and says all you have to do is "dump" everything into a Dutch oven and dinner is quick and easy for the second night in a row.

2 (14-oz.) cans chicken broth
2 cups frozen corn kernels
1 cup frozen baby lima beans
¹/₂ (20-oz.) package refrigerated diced potatoes with onions

3 cups Easy Barbecued Chicken (previous pages) or 1 lb. shredded chicken or pork
1 (8-oz.) can tomato sauce
¹/₄ tsp. salt
¹/₄ tsp. pepper

1. Combine first 4 ingredients in a Dutch oven over medium-high heat; bring to a boil. Reduce heat, and simmer 15 minutes, stirring occasionally.

2. Stir in Easy Barbecued Chicken and remaining ingredients; simmer 10 minutes.

Substitution note: Use 3 cups Easy Barbecued Chicken (previous pages) or about a pound of shredded chicken or pork barbecue from your favorite restaurant.

MENU IDEA FOR 4

- Marinated Chicken and Vegetable Kabobs
- Rice with green onions and cashews

GROCERIES NEEDED

Check staples: teriyaki sauce, soy sauce, olive oil, ground ginger, garlic powder, wooden skewers

- 6 (6-oz.) skinned and boned chicken breasts
- ²/₃ cup orange juice
- 2 medium-size red bell peppers
- 2 small red onions
- 1 (32-oz.) box converted rice
- 1 bunch green onions
- 1 small package unsalted cashews

PER ENTRÉE SERVING:
CALORIES 205 (22% from fat); FAT 5.1g (sat 0.9g, mono 2.9g, poly 0.8g); PROTEIN 31.1g; CARB 7.4g; FIBER 1g; CHOL 74mg; IRON 1.3mg; SODIUM 573mg; CALC 25mg

Prep: 26 min. ✳ **Cook:** 17 min. ✳ **Other:** 30 min.

Marinated Chicken and Vegetable Kabobs

Makes 8 kabobs (save 4 kabobs for recipe on following pages)

If you plan to make Easy Chicken Fried Rice, make extra rice today, and chill it so it will firm up for stir-frying.

6 (6-oz.) skinned and boned chicken breasts
²/₃ cup orange juice
3 Tbsp. teriyaki sauce
2 Tbsp. soy sauce
2 Tbsp. olive oil
1½ tsp. ground ginger
1½ tsp. garlic powder

8 (10-inch) wooden or metal skewers

2 medium-size red bell peppers, cut into 1½-inch pieces
2 small red onions, cut into wedges

1. Cut chicken into 1½-inch pieces. Combine orange juice and next 5 ingredients in a large zip-top freezer bag; add chicken. Seal and marinate in refrigerator 30 minutes, turning once.

2. Meanwhile, soak wooden skewers in water 30 minutes to prevent burning.

3. Preheat grill to medium-high (350° to 400°). Drain marinade from freezer bag into a small saucepan; bring to a boil, and boil 1 minute. Set aside.

4. Thread chicken alternately with peppers and onions onto skewers. Grill kabobs, covered, over medium-high heat 13 to 15 minutes or until done, turning occasionally and basting with reserved marinade.

Note about Planned-Overs: Cover and refrigerate 4 Marinated Chicken Kabobs to prepare Easy Chicken Fried Rice (following pages) up to 3 days later, if desired.

MENU IDEA FOR 6

- Easy Chicken Fried Rice
- Fortune cookies

GROCERIES NEEDED

Check staples: vegetable oil, large eggs, teriyaki sauce, soy sauce

Planned-overs needed: 4 Marinated Chicken and Vegetable Kabobs

- 1 (10-oz.) package frozen sweet peas
- 1 (32-oz.) box converted rice
- Chili-garlic sauce (optional)
- Fortune cookies

PER ENTRÉE SERVING:
CALORIES 447 (25% from fat);
FAT 12.5g (sat 2g, mono 5.7g,
poly 3.9g); PROTEIN 30.5g;
CARB 51g; FIBER 3.3g;
CHOL 120mg; IRON 3.5mg;
SODIUM 2065mg; CALC 52mg

Prep: 10 min. ❋ **Cook:** 10 min.

Easy Chicken Fried Rice

Makes 6 servings

"The great thing about this recipe is that it tastes better and takes less time than delivery. Not to mention that it saves money!"—Alana W., Erie, CO

4 Marinated Chicken and Vegetable Kabobs (previous pages)

3 Tbsp. vegetable oil, divided
2 large eggs, lightly beaten

1 (10-oz.) package frozen sweet peas, thawed
5 cups cooked long-grain rice
¼ cup teriyaki sauce
¼ cup soy sauce
1 tsp. chili-garlic sauce (optional)

1. Remove chicken and vegetables from skewers; cut into bite-size pieces. Set aside.

2. Heat 1 Tbsp. oil in a large nonstick skillet over medium-high heat; add eggs, and gently stir 1 minute or until soft scrambled. Remove eggs from skillet; cool and cut into bite-size pieces. Set aside.

3. Heat remaining 2 Tbsp. oil in skillet; add reserved chicken, vegetables, and peas; stir-fry 2 minutes. Add rice and remaining ingredients; stir-fry 5 minutes. Stir in reserved eggs.

Ingredient Note: Find chili-garlic sauce in a small jar alongside other Asian products in your grocer. It's concentrated, giving this recipe more authentic depth of flavor.

GROCERIES NEEDED

Check staples: sugar, paprika, ground cumin, ground cloves

- 1 (8-lb.) smoked fully cooked ham half
- 1 (12-oz.) can ginger ale
- 1 small jar molasses
- 1 small carton orange juice
- 1 orange (optional)
- 1 bunch fresh parsley (optional)
- 1 (6-oz.) package stuffing mix (such as Stove Top)
- 1 jar applesauce

PER ENTRÉE SERVING:
CALORIES 784 (45% from fat); FAT 39.1g (sat 17.1g, mono 12g, poly 1.1g); PROTEIN 62.1g; CARB 45.9g; FIBER 2.3g; CHOL 157mg; IRON 7.8mg; SODIUM 1744mg; CALC 507mg

Prep: 10 min. ❊ **Cook:** 2 hrs. ❊ **Other:** 10 min.

Baked Ham with Molasses Glaze

Makes 16 servings (chop 2 cups ham and save for recipe on following pages)

For generations, moms have appreciated the longevity and versatility of a home-baked ham. Freeze leftovers in 1 or 2 cup portions in airtight plastic bags up to 1 month for more easy meals.

2 Tbsp. sugar
1 Tbsp. paprika
1 tsp. ground cumin
½ tsp. ground cloves
1 (8-lb.) smoked fully cooked ham half, trimmed
1 (12-oz.) can ginger ale

½ cup molasses
⅓ cup orange juice
Garnish: orange wedges, parsley sprigs

1. Preheat oven to 350°. Combine first 4 ingredients. Score fat on ham in a diamond pattern. Rub sugar mixture over ham; place in a lightly greased shallow roasting pan. Pour ginger ale into pan.

2. Bake, covered, at 350° for 1 hour and 30 minutes.

3. Stir together molasses and orange juice; spoon over ham. Bake, uncovered, 30 more minutes. Let stand 10 minutes before slicing. Garnish, if desired. Serve with pan juices. Makes 16 servings.

Note about Planned-Overs: Cover and refrigerate 2 cups chopped Baked Ham with Molasses Glaze to prepare Ham-and-Pineapple Pizza (following pages) up to 5 days later, if desired.

MENU IDEA FOR 4

- Ham-and-Pineapple Pizza
- Carrot sticks and Ranch dressing

GROCERIES NEEDED

Check staples: olive oil, Ranch dressing

Planned-overs needed: 2 cups chopped Baked Ham with Molasses Glaze

- 1 (12-inch) refrigerated baked pizza crust
- 1 jar pizza sauce
- 1 (20-oz.) can pineapple tidbits
- 1 cup (4 oz.) shredded provolone cheese
- 1/2 cup (2 oz.) shredded mozzarella cheese
- 1 lb. carrots

PER 2 WEDGES: CALORIES 607 (36% from fat); FAT 24.3g (sat 9.2g, mono 4.9g, poly 0.7g); PROTEIN 32.6g; CARB 70g; FIBER 4.3g; CHOL 61mg; IRON 4mg; SODIUM 1683mg; CALC 420mg

Prep: 10 min. ❋ **Cook:** 10 min.

Ham-and-Pineapple Pizza

Makes 1 (12-inch) pizza

Your family will have no clue they're eating leftovers when they're cleverly presented in this trendy pizza.

1 (12-inch) refrigerated baked pizza crust
2 tsp. olive oil
1 cup pizza sauce
2 cups chopped Baked Ham with Molasses Glaze (previous pages)
1 (20-oz.) can pineapple tidbits, well drained
1 cup (4 oz.) shredded provolone cheese
1/2 cup (2 oz.) shredded mozzarella cheese

1. Preheat oven to 425°.

2. Brush pizza crust with olive oil. Spread pizza sauce evenly over crust, leaving a 1-inch margin. Top with ham and pineapple; sprinkle with shredded cheeses.

3. Bake at 425° for 10 minutes or until cheese melts and crust is lightly browned. Cut into 8 wedges.

Prep: 15 min. ❋ **Cook:** 1 hr., 50 min.

Italian Herb-Roasted Chicken

Makes 12 servings (cover and refrigerate 1 roasted chicken for recipe on following pages)

This recipe subtly introduces fresh herb flavors to children. If you prefer to use dried herbs instead of fresh, use a teaspoon each of dried rosemary, thyme, and oregano, and rub it evenly over the birds before roasting.

2 (4- to 5-lb.) roasting chickens
1 lemon, halved
2 Tbsp. olive oil
4 sprigs fresh rosemary
4 sprigs fresh thyme
4 sprigs fresh oregano
6 garlic cloves, peeled
½ tsp. salt
¼ tsp. pepper

1. Remove and discard giblets from chicken; rinse under cold water, and pat dry. Trim excess fat. Squeeze lemon juice over chicken, and rub with olive oil. Place 1 squeezed lemon half, 2 rosemary sprigs, 2 thyme sprigs, 2 oregano sprigs, and 3 garlic cloves into the cavity of each bird. Sprinkle with salt and pepper.

2. If desired, tie ends of legs together with heavy string. Lift wing tips up and under chicken. Place chickens, breast side up, on a rack in a shallow roasting pan. Bake at 375° for 1 hour and 50 minutes or until juices run clear or a meat thermometer inserted in thigh registers 180°.

Note about Planned-Overs: Cover and refrigerate 1 Italian Herb-Roasted Chicken to prepare Roasted Chicken and Pesto Panini (following pages) up to 3 days later, if desired.

MENU IDEA FOR 6

- Roasted Chicken and Pesto Panini
- Cherry tomatoes or tomato soup

GROCERIES NEEDED

Check staples: butter

Planned-overs needed: 1 Italian Herb-Roasted Chicken

- 1 (3.5-oz.) jar pesto sauce
- 1 loaf sliced sour-dough bread
- 1 (8-oz.) package provolone cheese slices
- 1 pt. cherry tomatoes or 3 (18.3-oz.) containers tomato soup (such as Campbell's Select)

PER ENTRÉE SERVING:
CALORIES 797 (55% from fat);
FAT 48.8g (sat 18.8g, mono 20g,
poly 6.3g); PROTEIN 55.5g;
CARB 31.8g; FIBER 2.2g;
CHOL 166mg; IRON 4.2mg;
SODIUM 1064mg; CALC 475mg

Prep: 10 min. ✳ **Cook:** 6 min.

Roasted Chicken and Pesto Panini

Makes 6 servings

Use a griddle or cook these sandwiches just as easily in a skillet, panini press, or one of those indoor electric grills so popular these days.

1 Italian Herb-Roasted Chicken (previous pages)

1 (3.5-oz.) jar pesto sauce
12 slices sourdough bread
1 (8-oz.) package provolone cheese slices
3 Tbsp. melted butter or margarine

1. Remove chicken from bones; shred into bite-size pieces. Discard bones.

2. Preheat griddle to 275°. Spread pesto sauce on 1 side of each bread slice. Arrange chicken and cheese on 6 bread slices. Top with remaining bread slices, pesto side down. Brush melted butter on both sides of each sandwich.

3. Place sandwiches on hot griddle, and press firmly with a large spatula. Cook 2 to 3 minutes on each side or until golden brown. Serve immediately.

Nutrition Note: To save over 50 calories per sandwich, omit the butter, and coat both sides of each sandwich with olive oil-flavored cooking spray before cooking.

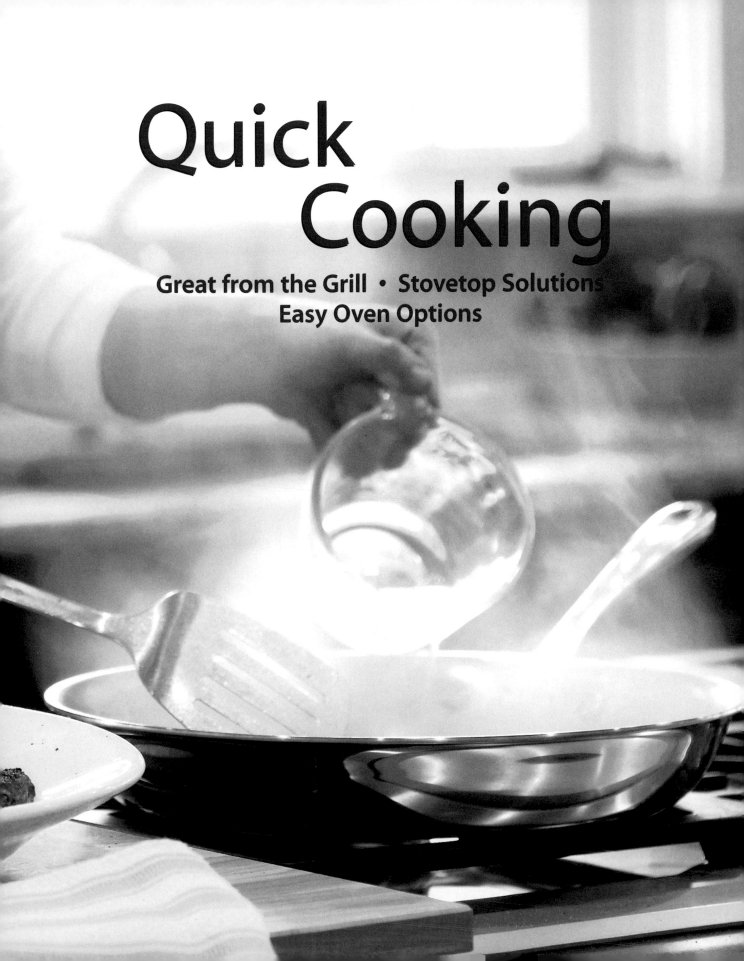

Quick Cooking

**Great from the Grill • Stovetop Solutions
Easy Oven Options**

Prep: 5 min. ✳ **Cook:** 12 min. ✳ **Other:** 10 min.

Caribbean Pork Chops with Apricot Sauce

Makes 4 servings

Using a spice rub is a great way to punch up the flavor when grilling ordinary meats. Let the kids rub or massage it into both sides of each chop. Be sure they wash their hands before and after applying the rub.

2 Tbsp. olive oil
1 Tbsp. brown sugar
1 tsp. chili paste
½ tsp. ground cumin
½ tsp. ground ginger
½ tsp. salt
½ tsp. pepper
4 (1-inch-thick) boneless pork loin chops

¼ cup mayonnaise
2 Tbsp. apricot preserves
1 tsp. fresh lemon juice
Dash of ground red pepper

1. Preheat grill to medium-high (350° to 400°). Stir together first 7 ingredients in a small bowl; rub evenly over both sides of pork chops. Let stand at room temperature 10 minutes.

2. Combine mayonnaise, apricot preserves, lemon juice, and red pepper in a small bowl; set aside.

3. Grill pork chops over medium-high heat 4 to 6 minutes on each side until pork is barely pink inside or a meat thermometer inserted into thickest portion registers 155°. Serve with apricot mixture.

Side Dish Note: Grill the pineapple slices over medium-high heat alongside the pork chops. Grill them only a minute or two on each side—just until you see nice grill marks.

172

Prep: 12 min. ❊ **Cook:** 30 min.

Barbecue Hobo Supper

Makes 4 servings

Easy cleanup is only one of the merits of cooking this one-dish meal in foil packets. It's also easier to customize each serving for picky eaters' tastes. Linda W., of Chesterfield, MO, recommends using a premium barbecue sauce. Her preference is Trader Joe's Organic.

1¹/₂ lb. ground round
¹/₂ cup barbecue sauce, divided
¹/₂ tsp. salt
¹/₂ tsp. pepper
1 lb. new potatoes, cut in half
¹/₂ lb. baby carrots
1 large red or green bell pepper, cut into 8 wedges
1 medium onion, cut into 8 wedges

1. Preheat grill to medium-high (350° to 400°). Tear off 4 (18- x 12-inch) rectangles of heavy-duty aluminum foil.

2. Combine ground round and ¹/₄ cup barbecue sauce; shape into 4 (¹/₂-inch-thick) patties. Place 1 patty in center of each foil sheet; sprinkle with salt and pepper. Spoon remaining ¹/₄ cup barbecue sauce over patties; surround with remaining ingredients. Bring up 2 sides of each aluminum foil sheet, and double fold with about 1-inch-wide folds. Double-fold each end to form a packet, leaving room for heat circulation inside packet.

3. Grill packets, covered with grill lid, over medium-high heat 12 to 15 minutes on each side or until beef is no longer pink and vegetables are tender. Carefully tear a small opening in each packet before serving to allow steam to escape.

Note: If the weather is not cooperating, cook this recipe indoors. Place foil packets on a baking sheet, and bake at 450° for 15 to 18 minutes on each side or until beef is no longer pink and vegetables are tender.

Prep: 15 min. ✳ Cook: 6 min.

Ham-and-Swiss Stuffed Burgers

Makes 4 servings

Lots of yummy stuff is inside this variation of the classic bacon cheeseburger. Buy the thinnest slices of ham and cheese you can find, and make sure the edges of the burgers are pinched together well so the cheese won't ooze out.

1 lb. ground round
1 Tbsp. Worcestershire sauce
¼ tsp. salt
¼ tsp. garlic powder
¼ tsp. pepper
2 (1-oz.) Swiss cheese slices
2 oz. thinly sliced deli ham

8 (1-oz.) slices sourdough bread
Toppings: lettuce leaves, red onion slices, tomato slices (optional)

1. Preheat grill to medium-high (350° to 400°). Combine first 5 ingredients; shape into 8 (5-inch) oval patties. Fold cheese slices into quarters and separate. Top 4 patties with 2 quarter slices cheese and ½ oz. ham, leaving a ½-inch border; top with remaining patties. Press edges together to seal.

2. Grill patties over medium-high heat 3 minutes on each side or until done. Meanwhile, place bread slices on grill rack; grill 1 minute on each side or until toasted. Serve burgers on toasted bread with desired toppings.

MENU IDEA FOR 6

- Grilled Ham and Apples
- Asian salad with sesame orange dressing
- Orange wedges

GROCERIES NEEDED

Check staples: butter, ground ginger

- 1 small jar orange marmalade
- 4 medium apples
- 2 (^{1}/$_2$-inch-thick) ham slices (about 2 lb.)
- 1 (11.4-oz.) package Asian salad kit (such as Fresh Express)
- 2 oranges

PER ENTRÉE SERVING:
CALORIES 432 (44% from fat); FAT 20.9g (sat 7.7g, mono 9.6g, poly 2.2g); PROTEIN 30.8g; CARB 30.5g; FIBER 2.4g; CHOL 85mg; IRON 1.3mg; SODIUM 2120mg; CALC 27mg

Prep: 5 min. ❈ **Cook:** 21 min.

Grilled Ham and Apples

Makes 6 servings

No need to core the apples in this recipe—just cut them into rings. As you do, let the kids see the star that holds the seeds.

½ cup orange marmalade
2 tsp. butter or margarine
¼ tsp. ground ginger

4 medium apples
2 (½-inch-thick) ham slices (about 2 lb.)

1. Preheat grill to medium-high (350° to 400°). Combine first 3 ingredients in a 1-cup glass measuring cup; microwave at HIGH 1 minute or until melted, stirring once.

2. Cut apples into ½-inch-thick rings. Grill ham and apples, covered with grill lid, over medium-high heat 20 minutes, turning and basting often with marmalade mixture. Cut ham slices into individual portions, and serve with apples.

Prep: 8 min. ✳ **Cook:** 20 min. ✳ **Other:** 30 min.

Honey-Grilled Butterflied Tenderloins

Makes 6 servings

A small amount of dark sesame oil gives the glaze a toasty, nutty flavor. It's one of the more perishable oils, so store it in the refrigerator up to 6 months. Write the purchase date on the label or lid with a permanent marker to refresh your memory.

2 (¾-lb.) pork tenderloins

¼ cup soy sauce
1 Tbsp. bottled minced garlic
½ tsp. ground ginger

2 Tbsp. brown sugar
3 Tbsp. honey
2 tsp. dark sesame oil
Garnish: fresh rosemary

1. Make a lengthwise cut down center of each tenderloin to within ¼ inch of opposite side; open tenderloin.

2. Combine soy sauce, garlic, and ginger in a large zip-top freezer bag; add tenderloins. Seal bag, and chill at least 30 minutes, turning occasionally.

3. Preheat grill to medium-high (350° to 400°). Stir together brown sugar, honey, and oil. Drain tenderloins, discarding marinade. Grill, covered with grill lid, over medium-high heat 10 minutes on each side or until pork is barely pink inside or a meat thermometer inserted into thickest portion registers 155°, basting often with honey mixture. Let stand 5 minutes or until temperature reaches 160°. Garnish, if desired.

Side Dish Note: Serve a warm vegetable salad alongside pork. Cut vegetables into large pieces, and grill alongside the pork until barely tender. Cool and cut them into bite-size pieces. Toss vegetables with a small amount of your favorite bottled vinaigrette.

Prep: 18 min. ✳ **Cook:** 8 min. ✳ **Other:** 5 min.

Steak Salad with Creamy Ranch Dressing

Makes 4 servings

A packaged salad "mix" typically contains shredded carrot and red cabbage in addition to the lettuce. Let the kids toss and plate the salad while an adult slices the steak.

MENU IDEA FOR 4

- Steak Salad with Creamy Ranch Dressing
- Vanilla ice cream

GROCERIES NEEDED

Check staples: garlic powder, brown sugar, ground red pepper, salt, pepper, Ranch dressing

- 1 (1-lb.) boneless sirloin steak (about ¹⁄₂ inch thick)
- 1 garlic bulb
- 1 loaf sliced sourdough bread
- 1 (16-oz.) bag classic iceberg salad mix (we tested with Dole's)
- 1 pt. grape tomatoes
- 1 small cucumber
- 1 small red onion
- Vanilla ice cream

PER ENTRÉE SERVING:
CALORIES 533 (59% from fat); FAT 35.1g (sat 9.9g, mono 8.2g, poly 1g); PROTEIN 27g; CARB 28g; FIBER 3.8g; CHOL 84mg; IRON 3.9mg; SODIUM 691mg; CALC 85mg

---

½ tsp. garlic powder
½ tsp. brown sugar
½ tsp. ground red pepper
¼ tsp. salt
¼ tsp. pepper
1 (1-lb.) boneless sirloin steak, trimmed (about ½ inch thick)

1 garlic clove, halved
4 (1-oz.) slices sourdough bread, toasted
1 (16-oz.) bag classic iceberg salad mix
1 pt. grape tomatoes
1 small cucumber, halved and sliced
1 small red onion, sliced
½ cup Ranch dressing

1. Preheat grill to medium-high (350° to 400°). Combine first 5 ingredients; rub evenly over both sides of steak.

2. Grill steak over medium-high heat 4 minutes on each side or until desired degree of doneness. Remove from heat; let stand 5 minutes. Cut steak diagonally across grain into thin slices.

3. Rub cut sides of garlic halves over toasted bread slices. Cut bread into ³⁄₄-inch cubes. Combine bread cubes, lettuce, tomatoes, cucumber, and onion in a large bowl. Add dressing, tossing gently to coat. Divide salad evenly among 4 plates; top with steak.

MENU IDEA FOR 4

- Halibut with Lemon Butter
- Yellow rice
- Grilled red bell peppers

GROCERIES NEEDED

Check staples: butter, dried Italian seasoning, salt, vegetable cooking spray, lemon pepper

- 1 bunch green onions
- 1 lemon
- 4 (6-oz.) halibut fillets
- 1 (10-oz.) package yellow rice
- 2 large red bell peppers

PER ENTRÉE SERVING:
CALORIES 325 (53% from fat); FAT 19.2g (sat 10.1g, mono 5.2g, poly 1.8g); PROTEIN 35.6g; CARB 0.8g; FIBER 0.1g; CHOL 95mg; IRON 1.5mg; SODIUM 503mg; CALC 88mg

Prep: 6 min. ❋ **Cook:** 10 min.

Halibut with Lemon Butter

Makes 4 servings

Use the Lemon Butter on beef, chicken, or any mild white fish. Buy extra lemons and teach the kids how to make lemonade by the glass.

⅓ cup butter or margarine, softened
1 green onion, minced
½ tsp. grated lemon rind
2 tsp. fresh lemon juice
½ tsp. dried Italian seasoning
½ tsp. salt

4 (6-oz.) halibut fillets
Vegetable cooking spray
½ tsp. lemon pepper

1. Preheat grill to medium-high (350° to 400°). Combine first 6 ingredients in a small bowl, stirring until well blended. Set lemon butter aside.

2. Coat fish with cooking spray, and sprinkle with lemon pepper. Place fillets on grill rack; grill, covered with grill lid, over medium-high heat 4 to 5 minutes on each side or until fish flakes with a fork. Serve with Lemon Butter.

Side Dish Note: Red, yellow, or orange bell peppers are sweeter than their green counterparts and much more appealing for younger palates. Cut them into quarters, and grill them alongside the fish at the same temperature and for the same amount of time. The results will be a juicy, tender, and lightly charred side dish.

MENU IDEA FOR 6

- Bistro Chicken Pizza
- Ranch salad

GROCERIES NEEDED

Check staples: heavy-duty aluminum foil, vegetable cooking spray, olive oil

- 1 (13.8-oz.) can refrigerated pizza crust dough
- 1 jar pizza sauce
- 4 plum tomatoes
- 2 cups chopped cooked chicken
- 1 (4-oz.) package tomato-and-basil feta cheese
- 1 cup (4 oz.) shredded mozzarella cheese
- 1 bunch fresh basil
- 2 (9.5-oz.) packages Ranch salad kit (such as Fresh Express Ranch)

PER ENTRÉE SERVING:
CALORIES 387 (34% from fat);
FAT 14.6g (sat 6.4g, mono 1.8g, poly 0.9g); PROTEIN 28.2g;
CARB 37.5g; FIBER 1g;
CHOL 65mg; IRON 2.7mg;
SODIUM 1008mg; CALC 156mg

Prep: 15 min. ❋ **Cook:** 10 min.

Bistro Chicken Pizza

Makes 6 servings

It's amazingly simple to cook pizza on the grill. Gather the ingredients as the grill preheats because once the grilling begins, you're about 10 minutes to dinner.

Vegetable cooking spray
1 (13.8-oz.) can refrigerated pizza crust dough
1 tsp. olive oil

¾ cup pizza sauce
4 plum tomatoes, sliced
2 cups chopped cooked chicken
1 (4-oz.) package tomato-and-basil feta cheese
1 cup (4 oz.) shredded mozzarella cheese
2 Tbsp. thinly sliced fresh basil

1. Preheat grill to medium (300° to 350°). Coat an 18- x 12-inch sheet of heavy-duty aluminum foil with cooking spray. Unroll dough onto aluminum foil; press out dough with hands to form a 13- x 9-inch rectangle. Brush evenly with olive oil.

2. Invert dough onto grill; peel off foil. Grill, covered with grill lid, over medium heat 2 to 3 minutes or until bottom of dough is browned. Turn dough over, and grill, covered, 1 to 2 minutes or until bottom is set. Carefully remove crust from grill to a baking sheet.

3. Spread pizza sauce evenly over crust; top with tomatoes and chicken. Sprinkle with cheeses and basil. Return pizza to grill. Grill, covered, 3 to 5 more minutes or until crust is done and cheese is melted.

Cooking Note: Use long-handled grilling tongs and a spatula to turn the dough on the grill with ease.

Prep: 17 min. ❋ **Cook:** 10 min. ❋ **Other:** 30 min.

Chicken Thighs with Thyme and Lemon

Makes 8 servings

"My daughter, Savannah, is a dancer and a healthy eater; however, she doesn't always eat very much. This is one wholesome recipe I can count on her to ask for seconds."—Mary B., Metairie, LA

½ tsp. grated lemon rind
1½ cups fresh lemon juice (about 10 lemons)
1 Tbsp. dried or 3 Tbsp. chopped fresh thyme
1 Tbsp. olive oil
3 Tbsp. honey
16 skinned and boned chicken thighs (about 3 lb.)

½ tsp. salt
¼ tsp. pepper

1. Place first 5 ingredients in a large zip-top freezer bag; add chicken. Seal bag, and chill at least 30 minutes, turning occasionally.

2. Preheat grill to medium-high (350° to 400°). Remove chicken from bag; discard marinade. Sprinkle chicken with salt and pepper; grill over medium-high heat 5 minutes on each side or until chicken is done.

Side Dish Note: Orzo is small, rice-shaped pasta that cooks up quickly. You'll find it alongside other dried pastas. Tossed with a few sweet peas, chopped fresh parsley, and some Parmesan cheese, it makes a perfect side dish for this healthy grilled entrée.

MENU IDEA FOR 8
- Chicken Thighs with Thyme and Lemon
- Orzo and peas
- Corn-on-the-cob

GROCERIES NEEDED

Check staples: dried thyme, olive oil, honey, salt, pepper, Parmesan cheese
- 10 lemons
- 16 skinned and boned chicken thighs (about 3 lb.)
- 1 (16-oz.) package orzo
- 1 (10-oz.) package frozen sweet peas
- 1 bunch fresh parsley
- 8 ears fresh corn

PER ENTRÉE SERVING:
CALORIES 272 (45% from fat); FAT 13.6g (sat 3.7g, mono 5.5g, poly 3g); PROTEIN 30.6g; CARB 5.5g; FIBER 0.3g; CHOL 112mg; IRON 1.8mg; SODIUM 249mg; CALC 20mg

MENU IDEA FOR 4

- Caramelized Onion Chicken
- Brown rice
- Roasted green beans

GROCERIES NEEDED

Check staples: salt, pepper, olive oil, red wine vinegar, soy sauce, bottled minced ginger, dried rosemary

- 1 lb. chicken breast tenders
- 1 small onion
- 1 small jar seedless raspberry jam
- 1 (14-oz.) box quick-cooking brown rice
- 1 lb. fresh green beans

PER ENTRÉE SERVING:
CALORIES 247 (9% from fat); FAT 2.6g (sat 0.6g, mono 1.2g, poly 0.5g); PROTEIN 26.9g; CARB 28.1g; FIBER 0.4g; CHOL 66mg; IRON 1mg; SODIUM 603mg; CALC 19mg

Prep: 7 min. ❋ **Cook:** 16 min.

Caramelized Onion Chicken

Makes 4 servings

Raspberry jam, red wine vinegar, soy sauce, and a couple of seasonings deglaze (loosen the browned bits of food) the skillet. Amye C. of Helena, AL, noted this recipe is low in fat, easy to whip together, and doesn't require purchasing lots of "extra" ingredients that she may never use again.

1 lb. chicken breast tenders
½ tsp. salt
¼ tsp. pepper
1 small onion, thinly sliced
1 tsp. olive oil

½ cup seedless raspberry jam
1 Tbsp. red wine vinegar
1 Tbsp. soy sauce
1 tsp. bottled minced ginger
½ tsp. dried rosemary

1. Sprinkle chicken with salt and pepper. Sauté onion in hot oil in a large skillet over medium-high heat 2 minutes. Add chicken to pan; cook 8 minutes or until chicken is done, turning occasionally. Remove onion and chicken from pan, and set aside.

2. Add jam and remaining ingredients to skillet; cook 2 minutes, stirring constantly with a whisk to loosen browned bits from skillet. Return chicken mixture to pan; cook 4 minutes, stirring occasionally.

Substitution Note: Red currant, apple, or seedless blackberry jam can stand in for raspberry jam with great results.

Prep: 5 min. ❋ **Cook:** 10 min.

Pork Chops with Dried Fruit

Makes 4 servings

Moms like Theda B. of Long Valley, NJ, have always counted on dried fruits as high-energy snacks for kids. Here, the natural sugars in the fruit provide a touch of sweetness that her two children love.

4 (6-oz.) bone-in pork chops (about
    $^1/_2$ inch thick)
$^1/_4$ tsp. salt
$^1/_4$ tsp. pepper
1 Tbsp. vegetable oil

$^1/_3$ cup chopped sweet onion or
   3 shallots, chopped
1 cup chicken broth
1 (7-oz.) package dried mixed fruit bits

1. Sprinkle both sides of pork with salt and pepper. Cook pork chops in hot oil in a large skillet over medium-high heat 3 minutes on each side or until lightly browned. Remove from pan, and set aside.

2. Add onion to pan; cook 1 minute, stirring constantly. Add broth and fruit to skillet; cook 1 minute, stirring to loosen browned bits from skillet. Return pork to pan, and cook 1 minute or until thoroughly heated.

MENU IDEA FOR 4

- Garlic-and-Herb Chicken Thighs
- Hot cooked rotini
- Tossed garden salad
- Dinner rolls

GROCERIES NEEDED

Check staples: all-purpose flour, salt, pepper, olive oil, balsamic vinegar, salad dressing

- 8 (4-oz.) skinned and boned chicken thighs
- 1 (14-oz.) can chicken broth or dry white wine
- 1 (10-oz.) can diced tomatoes and green chiles
- 1 (1.6-oz.) envelope garlic-and-herb sauce mix (we tested with Knorr)
- 1 bunch green onions
- 1 (8-oz.) package rotini
- 1 (16-oz.) bag romaine and iceberg salad mix
- 1 pt. grape tomatoes
- Dinner rolls

PER ENTRÉE SERVING:
CALORIES 492 (45% from fat); FAT 24.5g (sat 5.7g, mono 11.4g, poly 4.7g); PROTEIN 42.8g; CARB 17.5g; FIBER 1.4g; CHOL 151mg; IRON 3.1mg; SODIUM 1704mg; CALC 51mg

Prep: 12 min. ❊ **Cook:** 23 min.

Garlic-and-Herb Chicken Thighs

Makes 4 servings

The garlic-and-herb sauce mix can be found with the Italian sauce mixes on the pasta aisle of the grocery store.

¼ cup all-purpose flour
½ tsp. salt
½ tsp. pepper
8 (4-oz.) skinned and boned chicken thighs
2 Tbsp. olive oil

1 cup chicken broth or dry white wine
¼ cup balsamic vinegar
1 (10-oz.) can diced tomatoes and green chiles, undrained
1 (1.6-oz.) envelope garlic-and-herb sauce mix

4 green onions, sliced
Garnish: sliced green onion tops

1. Combine flour, salt, and pepper in a shallow dish; dredge chicken in flour mixture. Cook half of chicken in 1 Tbsp. oil in a large skillet over medium-high heat 4 minutes on each side or until lightly browned. Remove chicken from pan, and set aside. Repeat procedure with remaining chicken and oil.

2. Add broth and vinegar to skillet; cook 2 minutes, stirring to loosen browned bits from skillet. Stir in tomatoes and garlic-and-herb sauce mix until combined.

3. Return chicken to skillet. Cook, uncovered, over medium heat 5 minutes or until done. Stir in sliced green onions. Garnish, if desired.

MENU IDEA FOR 4

- Tuscan Pork Chops
- Couscous

GROCERIES NEEDED

Check staples: all-purpose flour, salt, seasoned pepper, olive oil, bottled minced garlic, balsamic vinegar

- 4 (1-inch-thick) boneless pork loin chops
- 1 (14-oz.) can chicken broth
- 3 plum tomatoes
- 1 jar capers
- 1 (10-oz.) box plain couscous

PER ENTRÉE SERVING:
CALORIES 433 (37% from fat); FAT 17.7g (sat 5.5g, mono 8.7g, poly 1.4g); PROTEIN 53g; CARB 12.2g; FIBER 0.8g; CHOL 141mg; IRON 2.1mg; SODIUM 820mg; CALC 65mg

Prep: 6 min. ✳ **Cook:** 11 min.

Tuscan Pork Chops

Makes 4 servings

These pork chops will be plenty juicy in the short amount of cooking time allotted here. Aim to have a little pink color in the meat when you're done.

¼ cup all-purpose flour
1 tsp. salt
¾ tsp. seasoned pepper
4 (1-inch-thick) boneless pork loin chops
1 Tbsp. olive oil

1½ tsp. bottled minced garlic
⅓ cup balsamic vinegar
⅓ cup chicken broth
3 plum tomatoes, seeded and diced
2 Tbsp. capers (optional)

1. Combine flour, salt, and pepper in a shallow dish; dredge pork chops in flour mixture. Cook pork chops in hot oil in a large skillet over medium-high heat 1 to 2 minutes on each side or until golden brown. Remove chops from pan, and set aside.

2. Add garlic to skillet, and sauté 1 minute. Add vinegar and broth to skillet; cook 1 minute, stirring to loosen browned bits from skillet. Stir in tomatoes and capers, if desired.

3. Return pork chops to skillet; bring to a boil. Cover, reduce heat, and simmer 4 to 5 minutes or until pork is done. Serve pork chops with tomato mixture.

MENU IDEA FOR 4

- Sesame-Orange Chicken
- Mesclun green salad
- French bread

GROCERIES NEEDED

Check staples: salt, ground red pepper, vegetable oil, butter, salad dressing

- 1 small jar sesame seeds
- 1 orange
- 4 (6-oz.) skinned and boned chicken breasts
- 1 (14-oz.) can chicken broth
- 1 small container orange juice
- 1 (8-oz.) container whipping cream
- 1 (16-oz.) package Mesclun greens
- 1 small loaf French bread

PER ENTRÉE SERVING:
CALORIES 279 (30% from fat); FAT 9.3g (sat 2.2g, mono 1.8g, poly 1.5g); PROTEIN 40.7g; CARB 4.2g; FIBER 0.2g; CHOL 109mg; IRON 7.8mg; SODIUM 648mg; CALC 24mg

Prep: 12 min. ❋ **Cook:** 18 min.

Sesame-Orange Chicken

Makes 4 servings

It just takes a minute or two to toast sesame seeds for this recipe. Here's how: Place a skillet over medium-high heat, and add sesame seeds. Cook, stirring constantly, 30 seconds or until the sesame seed aroma is obvious and the seeds are lightly toasted.

2 Tbsp. sesame seeds, toasted
1 Tbsp. grated orange rind
¼ tsp. salt, divided
Dash of ground red pepper

4 (6-oz.) skinned and boned chicken breasts
2 tsp. vegetable oil
1 tsp. butter or margarine

1 cup chicken broth
⅓ cup orange juice
1 Tbsp. whipping cream

1. Combine sesame seeds, orange rind, ⅛ tsp. salt, and pepper in a food processor; process until mixture resembles coarse meal.

2. Place chicken between 2 sheets of heavy-duty plastic wrap; pound to ¼-inch thickness, using a meat mallet or rolling pin. Sprinkle chicken evenly with remaining ⅛ tsp. salt. Heat oil and butter in a large skillet over medium heat until butter melts. Add chicken; cook 6 minutes on each side or until done. Remove chicken from pan; keep warm.

3. Add sesame mixture and broth to pan; bring to a boil. Cook 1 minute, stirring to loosen browned bits from skillet. Cook mixture about 3 minutes or until reduced to ⅔ cup. Add orange juice and cream; cook 30 seconds, stirring constantly. Serve sauce over chicken.

Side Salad Note: After removing grated rind from orange in Sesame-Orange Chicken, remove orange sections and add to salad.

MENU IDEA FOR 4

- Apricot Pork Chops
- Mashed potatoes
- Sugar snap peas

GROCERIES NEEDED

Check staples:
vegetable oil, bottled minced garlic, soy sauce

- 4 (4-oz.) boneless pork loin chops
- 1 small onion
- 1/3 cup apricot or peach preserves
- 1 bunch green onions (optional)
- 1 (24-oz.) package refrigerated mashed potatoes with skins
- 1 lb. sugar snap peas

PER ENTRÉE SERVING:
CALORIES 316 (42% from fat); FAT 14.8g (sat 4.5g, mono 6.5g, poly 2.3g); PROTEIN 25.7g; CARB 19.1g; FIBER 0.3g; CHOL 70mg; IRON 0.8mg; SODIUM 511mg; CALC 36mg

Prep: 5 min. ❊ Cook: 18 min.

Apricot Pork Chops

Makes 4 servings

"The green onions make these chops look pretty, but my daughter would just push them off to the side. So I just leave them out." —Doren H., Birmingham, AL

1 Tbsp. vegetable oil
4 (4-oz.) boneless pork loin chops

1/4 cup chopped onion
1 tsp. bottled minced garlic
1/3 cup apricot or peach preserves
2 Tbsp. soy sauce
2 green onions, sliced (optional)

1. Heat oil in a large skillet over medium-high heat. Add pork, and cook over medium-high heat 5 minutes on each side or until done. Remove from pan; keep warm.

2. Add onion and garlic to pan; cook 3 minutes or until tender. Add preserves and soy sauce; cook over medium-high heat 3 minutes, stirring to loosen browned bits from skillet. Return pork to pan, turning to coat. Sprinkle with green onions, if desired.

Doneness Tip: If you've ever wondered how to tell if a pork chop is done, you're not alone. Set your timer when you begin because these chops cook quickly. To test for doneness, press gently on the chop with your index finger. It should feel slightly firm but not hard.

Prep: 7 min. ☀ **Cook:** 19 min.

Superfast Salisbury Steak

Makes 6 servings

If you want to gradually introduce your family to ground turkey, prepare this recipe with 1 lb. ground chuck mixed with 1 lb. ground turkey. Most likely, they won't notice the difference.

2 lb. ground turkey or ground chuck
¹/₃ cup fine, dry breadcrumbs
1 large egg, lightly beaten
¹/₄ tsp. salt
¹/₄ tsp. pepper

Vegetable cooking spray

¹/₂ cup water
1 (10³/₄-oz.) can French onion soup
2 Tbsp. tomato paste
1 Tbsp. Worcestershire sauce

1. Combine first 5 ingredients. Shape mixture into 6 (¹/₂-inch-thick) oval-shaped patties.

2. Heat a large nonstick skillet coated with cooking spray over medium-high heat. Add patties; cook 3 minutes on each side or until browned. Remove patties from pan; keep warm. Drain pan, and wipe skillet with a paper towel to remove excess fat.

3. Add ¹/₂ cup water to pan; cook 1 minute, stirring to loosen browned bits from skillet. Add soup, tomato paste, and Worcestershire sauce; bring to a boil. Cook 3 minutes; reduce heat, and return patties to skillet. Cover and simmer 10 minutes.

Ingredient Note: Tomato paste in a tube works great for this recipe because you can easily refrigerate the remaining for other uses.

Prep: 5 min. ❋ **Cook:** 16 min.

Cider-Glazed Chicken with Dried Cranberries

Makes 4 servings

If you aren't a dried cranberry fan, try raisins instead. Use ¹/₃ cup or two of the little snack boxes moms often pack in kids' lunches.

1½ Tbsp. all-purpose flour
¾ tsp. salt
¼ tsp. ground allspice
4 (6-oz.) skinned and boned chicken breasts

1 Tbsp. butter or margarine

¹/₃ cup sweetened dried cranberries
½ cup apple cider or apple juice
1 Tbsp. cider vinegar or white balsamic vinegar

1. Combine flour, salt, and allspice in a zip-top freezer bag. Add chicken to bag; seal and shake to coat.

2. Melt butter in a large skillet over medium-high heat. Add chicken, and cook 4 minutes on each side or until done. Remove chicken from pan; keep warm.

3. Add cranberries, apple cider, and vinegar to pan; bring to a boil. Cook 3 minutes, stirring to loosen browned bits from skillet. Return chicken to pan, and cook 2 minutes or until thoroughly heated.

Freshness Note: Dried cranberries and raisins stay moist and retain their color, flavor, and nutrition when stored at 45° F for up to 5 months. Keep them in an airtight container in the coolest area of the refrigerator.

MENU IDEA FOR 4

- Cider-Glazed Chicken with Dried Cranberries
- Wild rice mix

GROCERIES NEEDED

Check staples: all-purpose flour, salt, ground allspice, butter, cider vinegar or white balsamic vinegar

- 4 (6-oz.) skinned and boned chicken breasts
- 1 (6-oz.) package sweetened dried cranberries (we tested with Ocean Spray Craisins)
- 1 small bottle apple cider or apple juice
- 1 (8.8-oz.) box quick-cooking wild rice mix

PER ENTRÉE SERVING:
CALORIES 272 (17% from fat); FAT 5.1g (sat 2.4g, mono 1.3g, poly 0.6g); PROTEIN 39.7g; CARB 14.1g; FIBER 0.7g; CHOL 106mg; IRON 1.5mg; SODIUM 567mg; CALC 21mg

MENU IDEA FOR 4

- Marmalade-Glazed Beef Patties
- Hot cooked rice
- Steamed yellow squash

GROCERIES NEEDED

Check staples: large egg; fine, dry bread-crumbs; prepared horseradish; soy sauce; lemon juice; bottled minced garlic

- 1 lb. ground chuck
- 1 (8-oz.) can water chestnuts
- 1 small jar orange marmalade
- 2 (8.8-oz.) packages microwaveable long-grain rice (such as Uncle Ben's Ready Rice)
- 1 lb. yellow squash

PER ENTRÉE SERVING:
CALORIES 541 (44% from fat); FAT 26.3g (sat 10.1g, mono 11g, poly 1.1g); PROTEIN 26.2g; CARB 50.6g; FIBER 2.8g; CHOL 136mg; IRON 3.3mg; SODIUM 1458mg; CALC 82mg

Prep: 10 min. ✳ **Cook:** 20 min.

Marmalade-Glazed Beef Patties

Makes 4 servings

Are you familiar with the saucy cocktail meatballs kids gravitate to at holiday parties? You'll find the same flavors including the tangy-sweet glaze in this recipe. Serve the beef patties over rice so no one will miss a drop.

1 lb. ground chuck
1 large egg
½ cup fine, dry breadcrumbs
2 Tbsp. prepared horseradish
1 (8-oz.) can water chestnuts, drained and diced

⅔ cup orange marmalade
½ cup water
¼ cup soy sauce
2 Tbsp. lemon juice
½ tsp. bottled minced garlic

1. Combine first 5 ingredients. Shape mixture into 4 patties.

2. Cook patties in a large nonstick skillet over medium-high heat 2 minutes on each side or until browned. Remove patties from pan; keep warm.

3. Drain pan, and wipe skillet with a paper towel to remove excess fat. Add orange marmalade and next 4 ingredients to skillet. Bring to a boil over medium heat; cook 6 minutes, stirring constantly to loosen browned bits from pan. Return patties to pan; reduce heat to low, and simmer 10 minutes.

- Maple-Glazed Salmon
- Buttered orzo
- Field greens with cherry tomatoes

GROCERIES NEEDED

Check staples: hoisin sauce, soy sauce, Dijon mustard, bottled minced garlic, ground red pepper, butter, salad dressing
- 1 small bottle maple syrup
- 4 (6-oz.) salmon fillets
- 1 (8-oz.) bag orzo
- 2 (8-oz.) packages field greens
- 1 pt. grape tomatoes

PER ENTRÉE SERVING:
CALORIES 308 (39% from fat); FAT 13.3g (sat 3.1g, mono 5.7g, poly 3.3g); PROTEIN 36.6g; CARB 7.8g; FIBER 0.2g; CHOL 87mg; IRON 0.7mg; SODIUM 305mg; CALC 27mg

Prep: 5 min. ✳ **Cook:** 10 min. ✳ **Chill:** 30 min.

Maple-Glazed Salmon

Makes 4 servings

"Everyone in my family loves salmon! In addition to being a high-quality protein source and low in saturated fat, it cooks quickly. That works for me." —Elsa-Maria L., Glen Allen, VA

3 Tbsp. hoisin sauce
3 Tbsp. maple syrup
1 Tbsp. soy sauce
1½ tsp. Dijon mustard
1 tsp. bottled minced garlic
⅛ tsp. ground red pepper

4 (6-oz.) salmon fillets

1. Whisk together first 6 ingredients in a small bowl. Place salmon in an 11- x 7-inch baking dish. Drizzle half of glaze over salmon, spreading to coat. Cover and chill 30 minutes. Set aside remaining glaze.

2. Preheat broiler.

3. Remove salmon from dish, discarding glaze. Place salmon, skin side down, on a lightly greased baking sheet. Broil 5 inches from heat 10 minutes or until fish flakes with a fork, brushing once after 5 minutes with reserved glaze.

Salmon Note: If the salmon skin is a turn off to youngsters, use a wide metal spatula to separate the fish from the skin, leaving it on the baking sheet.

MENU IDEA FOR 4

- Pimiento Cheese Chicken with Hot Buttered Grits
- Broiled tomatoes with breadcrumbs

GROCERIES NEEDED

Check staples:
seasoned salt; pepper; butter; fine, dry breadcrumbs

- 4 (6-oz.) skinned and boned chicken breasts
- 1 tub premium-quality pimiento cheese (we tested with Mrs. Stratton's Premium Gold)
- 1 (32-oz.) container chicken broth (we tested with Swanson)
- 1 (8.4-oz.) box quick-cooking grits (we tested with Quaker)
- 4 plum or small tomatoes

PER ENTRÉE SERVING:
CALORIES 599 (29% from fat); FAT 19.4g (sat 10.2g, mono 2.2g, poly 1g); PROTEIN 49.2g; CARB 50.5g; FIBER 1.1g; CHOL 154mg; IRON 3.3mg; SODIUM 2128mg; CALC 31mg

Prep: 6 min. ❄ **Cook:** 17 min.

Pimiento Cheese Chicken with Hot Buttered Grits

Makes 4 servings

"My kids love pimiento cheese when it's slathered and melted on an ordinary chicken breast. Sometimes we jazz it up by stirring chopped jalapeño peppers or crumbled bacon into the pimiento cheese." —Elizabeth A., Test Kitchens Director

4	(6-oz.) skinned and boned chicken breasts
½	tsp. seasoned salt
¼	tsp. pepper
¾	cup premium-quality pimiento cheese
4	cups chicken broth
1⅓	cups uncooked quick-cooking grits
2	Tbsp. butter or margarine

1. Preheat broiler. Place chicken between 2 sheets of heavy-duty plastic wrap, and flatten to ¼-inch thickness, using a meat mallet or rolling pin. Sprinkle chicken with salt and pepper; place chicken on a lightly greased rack in a broiler pan.

2. Broil chicken 5 inches from heat 5 minutes. Turn chicken, and spoon 3 Tbsp. pimiento cheese over each chicken breast, spreading to edges. Broil 5 more minutes or until cheese is bubbly and lightly browned.

3. Bring chicken broth to a boil in a large saucepan over medium-high heat. Reduce heat to low; whisk in grits. Cover and cook 5 to 7 minutes or until thickened, stirring occasionally. Remove from heat, and stir in butter. Serve with chicken.

Shopping Note: Find the best quality pimiento cheese in the deli section of your supermarket where it's available by weight or in prepackaged tubs. It has more Cheddar cheese and less processed cheese than many lower priced varieties.

Prep: 8 min. ❈ **Cook:** 12 min. ❈ **Other:** 35 min.

Southwestern Flank Steak with Corn Salsa

Makes 6 servings

Serve the Corn Salsa in a small dish on the side for those who prefer keeping their foods distinctly separate.

1 (1½-lb.) flank steak
2 Tbsp. fajita seasoning

¼ cup fresh lime juice
1 Tbsp. vegetable oil
2 cups frozen whole kernel corn, thawed
½ cup chopped red onion
½ cup chopped red bell pepper
¼ cup chopped fresh cilantro
¾ tsp. salt
¼ tsp. ground red pepper

1. Preheat broiler. Rub both sides of flank steak with seasoning. Place in a large zip-top plastic bag; seal and chill 30 minutes.

2. Meanwhile, combine lime juice and oil in a small bowl; stir in next 6 ingredients. Cover and chill until ready to serve.

3. Place steak on a lightly greased rack in a broiler pan. Broil 5 inches from heat 6 minutes on each side or to desired degree of doneness. Let stand 5 minutes before slicing. Cut steak diagonally across grain into thin slices. Serve with corn salsa.

Seasoning Note: Fajita seasoning is a zesty blend of savory spices, but it's not spicy.

Green Chile Broiled Tilapia

Menu Idea for 6 {#menu}

Makes 6 servings

Squeeze fresh lime juice over fish at the table to bring out the brightest flavor. And while you're at it, show the kids how to squeeze lime wedges on their food and not squirt the juice elsewhere!

MENU IDEA FOR 6
- Green Chile Broiled Tilapia
- Mexican rice

GROCERIES NEEDED

Check staples: salt, pepper, ketchup, olive oil, ground cumin, hot sauce
- 6 (6-oz.) tilapia or orange roughy fillets
- 1 (4.5-oz.) can chopped green chiles
- 2 limes
- 2 (5.4-oz.) packages Mexican rice (such as Lipton Fiesta Sides)

PER ENTRÉE SERVING:
CALORIES 197 (24% from fat); FAT 5.3g (sat 1.3g, mono 2.6g, poly 0.9g); PROTEIN 34.3g; CARB 3.3g; FIBER 0.2g; CHOL 85mg; IRON 1.1mg; SODIUM 362mg; CALC 22mg

6 (6-oz.) tilapia or orange roughy fillets
1/2 tsp. salt
1/4 tsp. pepper

1 (4.5-oz.) can chopped green chiles
2 Tbsp. ketchup
1 Tbsp. olive oil
1 tsp. grated lime rind
1 Tbsp. fresh lime juice
1/4 tsp. ground cumin
1/8 to 1/4 tsp. hot sauce

Lime wedges

1. Preheat broiler. Sprinkle fillets with salt and pepper. Arrange fillets on a lightly greased rack in a broiler pan.

2. Stir together green chiles and next 6 ingredients in a small bowl. Spoon about half of mixture evenly over fillets, spreading to edges.

3. Broil 5 inches from heat 10 minutes or until fish flakes with a fork. Serve fish with remaining green chile mixture and lime wedges.

MENU IDEA FOR 4

- Crisp Lemon-Pepper Catfish
- Long-grain and wild rice
- Steamed asparagus

GROCERIES NEEDED

Check staples: vegetable cooking spray, all-purpose flour, lemon pepper, salt

- 4 (6-oz.) catfish fillets
- 2 lemons
- 1 small package panko (Japanese breadcrumbs)
- 2 (8.8-oz.) packages microwaveable long-grain and wild rice (such as Uncle Ben's Ready Rice)
- 1 lb. fresh asparagus

PER ENTRÉE SERVING:
CALORIES 282 (43% from fat); FAT 13.5g (sat 3g, mono 6.1g, poly 2.7g); PROTEIN 28g; CARB 10.6g; FIBER 0.5g; CHOL 80mg; IRON 1mg; SODIUM 295mg; CALC 18mg

Prep: 10 min. ✳ **Cook:** 10 min.

Crisp Lemon-Pepper Catfish

Makes 4 servings

"My 10-year-old son assembled this recipe all by himself. All I had to do was oversee the broiling process." —Lori G., Apopka, FL

4 (6-oz.) catfish fillets
Vegetable cooking spray
2 tsp. fresh lemon juice

½ cup panko (Japanese breadcrumbs)
2 Tbsp. all-purpose flour
2 tsp. lemon pepper
¼ tsp. salt

Lemon wedges

1. Preheat broiler. Coat both sides of fish with cooking spray; drizzle with lemon juice.

2. Combine breadcrumbs, flour, lemon pepper, and salt in a shallow dish. Dredge fish in breadcrumb mixture.

3. Place fish on a lightly greased rack in a broiler pan. Broil 5 inches from heat 10 minutes or until fish flakes with a fork. Serve with lemon wedges.

Ingredient Note: Panko, crunchy Japanese breadcrumbs, make this crust extra crisp. Find the product with other Asian foods at your grocer.

MENU IDEA FOR 4

- Broiled Steaks with Mushrooms
- Baked potatoes
- Cucumber and tomato salad

GROCERIES NEEDED

Check staples: salt, pepper, garlic powder, butter, bottled vinaigrette

- 4 (12-oz.) rib-eye or chuck-eye beef steaks (1 inch thick)
- 1 (8-oz.) package sliced fresh mushrooms
- 1 bunch fresh parsley (optional)
- 4 baking potatoes
- 1 cucumber
- 2 large tomatoes

PER ENTRÉE SERVING:
CALORIES 709 (59% from fat);
FAT 46.6g (sat 19.4g, mono 18.1g,
poly 1.8g); PROTEIN 66.5g;
CARB 2.3g; FIBER 0.7g;
CHOL 321mg; IRON 4.8mg;
SODIUM 826mg; CALC 49mg

Prep: 15 min. ❄ **Cook:** 14 min.

Broiled Steaks with Mushrooms

Makes 4 servings

The second to the top shelf of an oven is typically 5 inches from the broiler. If your shelf is any closer, the cook time likely will be less.

4 (12-ounce) rib-eye or chuck-eye beef steaks (1 inch thick)
1⅛ tsp. salt, divided
½ tsp. pepper
½ tsp. garlic powder

2 Tbsp. butter or margarine
1 (8-oz.) package sliced fresh mushrooms
Garnish: chopped fresh parsley

1. Preheat broiler. Sprinkle steaks with 1 tsp. salt, pepper, and garlic powder. Place steaks on a lightly greased rack in a broiler pan.

2. Broil 5 inches from heat 6 to 7 minutes on each side or to desired degree of doneness.

3. Melt butter in a small saucepan over medium-high heat; add mushrooms. Sauté 3 minutes or until lightly browned; stir in remaining ⅛ tsp. salt. Serve mushroom mixture with steaks. Garnish, if desired.

Equipment Substitution: If you don't have a broiler pan with a rack, use a cooling rack inside a jelly-roll pan.

MENU IDEA FOR 4

- Crisp Garlic Chicken
- Angel hair pasta with marinara sauce
- Mixed greens with oil and vinegar

GROCERIES NEEDED

Check staples: bottled minced garlic, olive oil, Italian-seasoned breadcrumbs, grated Parmesan cheese, pepper, salad vinegar

- 4 (6-oz.) skinned and boned chicken breasts
- 1 (16-oz.) package angel hair pasta (such as Barilla)
- 1 (26-oz.) jar marinara sauce
- 1 (16-oz.) package mixed greens

PER ENTRÉE SERVING:
CALORIES 339 (36% from fat);
FAT 13.5g (sat 2.5g, mono 7.8g,
poly 1.5g); PROTEIN 42g;
CARB 9.9g; FIBER 0.5g;
CHOL 102mg; IRON 1.9mg;
SODIUM 518mg; CALC 85mg

Prep: 9 min. ✳ **Cook:** 25 min.

Crisp Garlic Chicken

Makes 4 servings

"My kids love chicken, love garlic, and love anything crisp, so this recipe is a grand slam at my house." —Kimberly D., Boxford, MA

1 tsp. bottled minced garlic
¼ cup olive oil

¾ cup Italian-seasoned breadcrumbs
¼ cup grated Parmesan cheese
¼ tsp. pepper
4 (6-oz.) skinned and boned chicken breasts

1. Preheat oven to 425°. Combine garlic and olive oil in a small microwave-safe bowl; microwave at HIGH 30 to 45 seconds or just until warm.

2. Combine breadcrumbs, cheese, and pepper in a shallow dish. Dip chicken in warm olive oil; dredge in breadcrumb mixture. Place chicken on a lightly greased baking sheet.

3. Bake at 425° for 20 to 25 minutes or until chicken is golden.

Prep: 20 min. ✳ **Cook:** 1 hr.

Bacon-Wrapped Chicken Thighs

Makes 8 servings

"This recipe has all the flavor and crunch of a homestyle fried chicken with less effort and none of the mess. I love the short list of ingredients." —Melissa C., Alpharetta, GA

MENU IDEA FOR 8
- Bacon-Wrapped Chicken Thighs
- Deli pasta salad
- Watermelon wedges

GROCERIES NEEDED

Check staples: cornmeal, paprika, salt, pepper
- 1 (12-oz.) package bacon
- 8 (4-oz.) skinned and boned chicken thighs
- 2 lb. deli pasta salad
- 1 small watermelon

PER ENTRÉE SERVING:
CALORIES 240 (43% from fat); FAT 11.4g (sat 3.3g, mono 4.5g, poly 2.4g); PROTEIN 23.7g; CARB 9g; FIBER 1.1g; CHOL 81mg; IRON 2mg; SODIUM 561mg; CALC 52mg

8 bacon slices

1 cup cornmeal
1 tsp. paprika
1 tsp. salt
1 tsp. pepper
8 (4-oz.) skinned and boned chicken thighs

1. Arrange bacon slices on paper towels on a microwave-safe plate; top with a paper towel. Microwave at HIGH 1 minute or just until bacon is limp and heated through. (Do not fully cook bacon.)

2. Preheat oven to 350°. Combine cornmeal and next 3 ingredients in a bowl. Dredge chicken thighs in cornmeal mixture. Wrap each thigh with a piece of bacon; secure with a wooden pick, if desired. Place chicken on a lightly greased rack in a broiler pan.

3. Bake at 350° for 50 minutes to 1 hour or until chicken is done.

MENU IDEA FOR 6

- Easy Chicken Cordon Bleu
- Pasta
- Chopped romaine with strawberries and French dressing

GROCERIES NEEDED

Check staples: grated Parmesan cheese, large eggs, salt, pepper

- 1 (5.5-oz.) box seasoned croutons (we tested with Pepperidge Farm)
- 6 (6-oz.) skinned and boned chicken breasts
- 6 (1-oz.) cooked ham slices
- 6 (1-oz.) Swiss cheese slices
- 1 bottle honey mustard dressing (optional)
- 1 lb. pasta
- 1 (16-oz.) package romaine lettuce
- 1 pt. strawberries
- 1 bottle French dressing

PER ENTRÉE SERVING:
CALORIES 469 (32% from fat); FAT 16.7g (sat 7.6g, mono 5.6g, poly 1.2g); PROTEIN 58.3g; CARB 17.6g; FIBER 0g; CHOL 140mg; IRON 1.5mg; SODIUM 1038mg; CALC 348mg

Prep: 15 min. ❋ **Cook:** 25 min.

Easy Chicken Cordon Bleu

Makes 6 servings

"The Cordon Bleu recipe I've always used calls for frying the chicken. This recipe was oven-fried and there was no sacrifice in taste. It will definitely become one of our standby recipes." —Holly B., Alabaster, AL

1 (5.5-oz.) box seasoned croutons, finely crushed
1/3 cup grated Parmesan cheese
2 egg whites
2 Tbsp. water
1/2 tsp. salt
1/4 tsp. pepper
6 (6-oz.) skinned and boned chicken breasts

6 (1-oz.) cooked ham slices
6 (1-oz.) Swiss cheese slices
Honey mustard dressing (optional)

1. Preheat oven to 450°. Combine crouton crumbs and Parmesan cheese in a large zip-top plastic bag; seal and shake well. Whisk together egg whites and 2 Tbsp. water in a shallow bowl. Sprinkle salt and pepper over chicken. Dip 1 chicken breast in egg white mixture; place in plastic bag. Seal and shake to coat. Place chicken on a lightly greased rack in a broiler pan. Repeat procedure with remaining chicken, egg white mixture, and crouton mixture.

2. Bake at 450° for 20 minutes. Top each breast with 1 ham slice and 1 Swiss cheese slice. Bake 5 more minutes or until cheese melts. Serve with honey mustard dressing, if desired.

Preparation Tip: A food processor makes crushing the croutons quick. For another easy way, place them in a large zip-top plastic bag and remove as much air as possible. Seal the bag and place it on the countertop. Pound the bag using a rolling pin or heavy can. Kids love to do this.

MENU IDEA FOR 4

- Crispy Onion Baked Chicken
- Roasted potato wedges
- Tossed green salad

GROCERIES NEEDED

Check staples: fine, dry breadcrumbs; mayonnaise; salad dressing

- 1 (1.4-oz.) package dry onion soup mix
- 4 (6-oz.) skinned and boned chicken breasts
- 1 (24-oz.) package frozen roasted potato wedges with skins (such as Ore-Ida)
- 1 (10-oz.) package spring mix (such as Fresh Express)

PER ENTRÉE SERVING:
CALORIES 409 (39% from fat); FAT 17.9g (sat 2.8g, mono 0.7g, poly 0.9g); PROTEIN 42.1g; CARB 17g; FIBER 1.2g; CHOL 105mg; IRON 2.2mg; SODIUM 937mg; CALC 65mg

Prep: 10 min. ❄ **Cook:** 25 min.

Crispy Onion Baked Chicken

Makes 4 servings

Moms love the easy shake-and-bake technique using only 4 common ingredients. The dry onion soup mixed with breadcrumbs adds crunch and the mayonnaise holds it in place.

1   cup fine, dry breadcrumbs
1   (1.4-oz.) package dry onion soup mix
4   (6-oz.) skinned and boned chicken breasts
⅓   cup mayonnaise

1. Preheat oven to 425°.

2. Combine breadcrumbs and soup mix in a large zip-top freezer bag; seal and shake well.

3. Brush 1 chicken breast with mayonnaise; place in plastic bag. Seal and shake to coat. Place chicken on an ungreased rack in a broiler pan. Repeat procedure with remaining chicken, mayonnaise, and breadcrumb mixture. Bake at 425° for 20 to 25 minutes or until chicken is lightly browned.

Great New Flavors

Best in the World · **Anyway You Like It**
For Kids Who Dare!

Prep: 18 min. ❄ **Cook:** 8 min.

Asian Chicken Burgers with Peanut Sauce

Makes 4 servings

We are amazed at how many Moms tell us their families like to venture out and taste kid-friendly versions of new ethnic recipes like this one and the ones to follow. These Asian burgers do sport a little heat thanks to the chile paste and ginger. Cool, crisp lettuce leaves provide a good balance.

1 lb. skinned and boned chicken breasts, coarsely chopped
4 green onions, chopped
1 Tbsp. chile paste with garlic
1 tsp. grated peeled fresh ginger
2 tsp. soy sauce
¼ tsp. salt

4 (2-oz.) sandwich rolls with sesame seeds
4 lettuce leaves, thinly sliced
Bottled peanut sauce (optional)

1. Preheat grill to medium (300° to 350°). Combine chicken, green onions, chile paste, ginger, soy sauce, and salt in a food processor; process until coarsely ground. Divide mixture into 4 equal portions; shape each portion into a ½-inch-thick patty.

2. Grill patties over medium heat 4 minutes on each side or until done. Meanwhile, place sandwich rolls, cut sides down, on grill rack; grill 1 minute or until toasted. Serve patties on sandwich rolls with lettuce and peanut sauce, if desired.

Prep: 8 min. ✳ Cook: 18 min.

Santa Fe Pizza

Makes 4 servings

"Pork sausage has a longer refrigerator life than ground beef, so I can shop for this recipe a week ahead. To make it super quick, I leave out the red bell pepper and jalapeño pepper and serve it with hot salsa." —Whitney P., Laurel, MS

½ (1-lb.) package ground mild or hot pork sausage
½ cup finely chopped red bell pepper
1 Tbsp. finely chopped pickled jalapeño pepper (optional)

1 (14-oz.) package prebaked Italian pizza crust
1 cup chunky salsa
1 tsp. chili powder
½ cup canned black beans, drained and rinsed
1 cup (4 oz.) shredded Cheddar-Monterey Jack cheese blend

½ cup sour cream (optional)
Garnish: cilantro sprigs

1. Preheat oven to 450°. Cook sausage in a large skillet over medium-high heat, stirring until it crumbles and is no longer pink. Drain and pat dry with paper towels. Wipe skillet clean. Return sausage to skillet. Add bell pepper and jalapeño pepper, if desired; cook 3 minutes or until tender.

2. Place pizza crust on a baking sheet. Bake at 450° for 8 minutes. Combine salsa and chili powder; spread over warm crust. Top with sausage mixture and black beans; sprinkle with cheese.

3. Bake at 450° for 6 minutes or until cheese melts. Cut into 8 wedges. Serve with sour cream, if desired. Garnish, if desired.

Table Talk: This is an example of *fusion* cuisine kids will understand. An Italian pizza crust anchors south-of-the-border toppings in a family-friendly main dish.

MENU IDEA FOR 4
• Santa Fe Pizza
• Tossed salad

GROCERIES NEEDED

Check staples: chunky salsa, chili powder, salad dressing
• 1 (1-lb.) package ground mild or hot pork sausage
• 1 small red bell pepper
• 1 jar pickled jalapeño peppers (optional)
• 1 (14-oz.) package prebaked Italian pizza crust (we tested with Boboli)
• 1 (15-oz.) can black beans
• 1 cup (4 oz.) shredded Cheddar-Monterey Jack cheese blend
• 1 (8-oz.) container sour cream (optional)
• 1 bunch fresh cilantro (optional)
• 1 (16-oz.) package iceberg lettuce with shredded carrots

PER 2 WEDGES: CALORIES 636 (48% from fat); FAT 33.7g (sat 12.7g, mono 6.8g, poly 2.1g); PROTEIN 25.2g; CARB 59.9g; FIBER 5.5g; CHOL 66mg; IRON 4.3mg; SODIUM 1364mg; CALC 121mg

MENU IDEA FOR 4

- Roasted Red Pepper-Caesar Tortelloni
- Raspberry sorbet

GROCERIES NEEDED

Check staples: Dijon mustard, pepper

- 2 (8-oz.) packages dried tortelloni (we tested with Barilla)
- 1 bottle creamy Caesar dressing (we tested with Wishbone)
- 1 lemon
- 1 jar roasted red bell peppers
- 1 package Caesar-style croutons
- ¹/₂ gal. raspberry sorbet

PER ENTRÉE SERVING:
CALORIES 549 (45% from fat);
FAT 27.2g (sat 8.7g, mono 4.5g,
poly 9.6g); PROTEIN 16.7g;
CARB 59.1g; FIBER 3.3g;
CHOL 63mg; IRON 3.1mg;
SODIUM 1736mg; CALC 275mg

Prep: 15 min. ❈ **Cook:** 15 min.

Roasted Red Pepper-Caesar Tortelloni

Makes 4 servings

"Once you make this recipe, you'll likely be able to whip it up from memory. My son suggested adding chunks of roasted chicken. We tried that and thought it was yummy!"—Kimberly D., Boxford, MA

2 (8-oz.) packages dried tortelloni

1 cup bottled creamy Caesar dressing
¹/₂ tsp. grated lemon rind
2 tsp. fresh lemon juice
¹/₂ tsp. Dijon mustard
¹/₄ tsp. pepper

¹/₂ cup jarred roasted red bell peppers, cut into thin strips
³/₄ cup Caesar-style croutons

1. Cook pasta according to package directions; drain.

2. Meanwhile, combine dressing and next 4 ingredients in a small microwave-safe bowl. Microwave at MEDIUM (50% power) 45 seconds to 1 minute or until warm, stirring after 30 seconds.

3. Combine hot cooked pasta and red pepper strips in a large bowl. Pour dressing mixture evenly over pasta mixture, tossing to coat. Divide mixture evenly among 4 serving bowls; top with croutons.

Substitution Note: Italian tortelloni are larger than bite-sized tortellini and come in a variety of fillings like cheese and garlic, porcini mushroom, and ricotta and spinach. Substituting an equal weight of tortellini works fine, too.

Greek Chicken Breasts

Makes 4 servings

"The two pantry items I'm never without are canned tomatoes and orzo. The tomatoes offer fresh flavor anytime of the year, and the orzo has great texture and cooks incredibly fast. My kids prefer it over rice or potatoes any day." —Retta J., Orlando, FL

¼ cup all-purpose flour
1 Tbsp. dried oregano
½ tsp. salt
4 (6-oz.) skinned and boned chicken breasts

3 Tbsp. olive oil
1 (14.5-oz.) can diced tomatoes with garlic and onion, undrained
⅓ cup chicken broth or dry white wine
1 (2.25-oz.) can sliced ripe olives, drained
2 Tbsp. capers
¼ cup crumbled feta cheese

1. Combine flour, oregano, and salt in a shallow dish; dredge chicken breasts in flour mixture.

2. Heat oil in a large skillet over medium-high heat until hot. Add chicken, and cook 4 minutes on each side or until browned. Drain well, and return chicken to pan. Add tomatoes and broth; reduce heat, and simmer 10 to 15 minutes. Add olives and capers; cook until thoroughly heated. Sprinkle with feta cheese.

Table Talk: Tell the kids orzo is a pasta just like spaghetti but it's shaped like rice. Capers are flower buds picked from a Mediterranean bush. Feta cheese is a classic Greek cheese that doesn't shred—it crumbles.

MENU IDEA FOR 4
- Greek Chicken Breasts
- Orzo
- Green beans

GROCERIES NEEDED

Check staples: all-purpose flour, dried oregano, salt, olive oil

- 4 (6-oz.) skinned and boned chicken breasts
- 1 (14.5-oz.) can diced tomatoes with garlic and onion
- ⅓ cup chicken broth or dry white wine
- 1 (2.25-oz.) can sliced ripe olives
- 1 small jar capers
- 1 oz. crumbled feta cheese
- 1 (8-oz.) package orzo
- 1 (16-oz.) package frozen green beans

PER ENTRÉE SERVING:
CALORIES 378 (38% from fat); FAT 16.1g (sat 3.5g, mono 8.8g, poly 1.7g); PROTEIN 43.5g; CARB 14.4g; FIBER 1.8g; CHOL 108mg; IRON 4.1mg; SODIUM 1316mg; CALC 107mg

Guacamole-and-Asadero-Topped Chicken

Makes 4 servings

"It's easier to get my young boys involved when I cook on the stove versus the oven because they can see the chicken sizzle and smell the aroma. They both help pound the chicken and measure the ingredients." —Hope M., Saltillo, MS

MENU IDEA FOR 4

- Guacamole-and-Asadero-Topped Chicken
- Black beans
- Papaya wedges

GROCERIES NEEDED

Check staples: vegetable oil, cider vinegar, Dijon mustard, onion powder, bottled minced garlic, salt, pepper

- 4 (6-oz.) skinned and boned chicken breasts
- 3 limes
- ³/₄ cup (3 oz.) shredded Asadero or Monterey Jack cheese
- 1 (8-oz.) package refrigerated, vacuum-packed, prepared guacamole (we tested with Avo Classic)
- 1 (8-oz.) container sour cream
- 1 tomato and/or 1 bunch cilantro (optional)
- 2 (15-oz.) cans black beans
- 1 large papaya

PER ENTRÉE SERVING:
CALORIES 491 (57% from fat); FAT 30.9g (sat 8.5g, mono 7.7g, poly 5.4g); PROTEIN 45.1g; CARB 6.4g; FIBER 2.3g; CHOL 127mg; IRON 2.2mg; SODIUM 513mg; CALC 177mg

4 (6-oz.) skinned and boned chicken breasts

¼ cup vegetable oil, divided
2 Tbsp. cider vinegar
1 Tbsp. fresh lime juice
1 Tbsp. Dijon mustard
½ tsp. onion powder
½ tsp. bottled minced garlic
¼ tsp. salt
¼ tsp. pepper

2 lime wedges
¾ cup (3 oz.) shredded Asadero or Monterey Jack cheese

1 (8-oz.) package refrigerated, vacuum-packed, prepared guacamole
¼ cup sour cream
Toppings: chopped tomato, chopped cilantro (optional)
Lime wedges (optional)

1. Place chicken breasts between 2 sheets of heavy-duty plastic wrap, and pound to ¼-inch thickness, using a rolling pin.

2. Combine 2 Tbsp. oil and next 7 ingredients in a large zip-top freezer bag; add chicken. Seal bag, and chill 30 minutes, turning once.

3. Drain chicken, discarding marinade; pat dry with paper towels. Heat remaining 2 Tbsp. oil in a large skillet over medium-high heat. Add chicken, and cook 5 minutes on each side or until done. Squeeze 2 lime wedges over chicken; top with cheese. Cover and cook 2 minutes or until cheese melts.

4. Stir together guacamole and sour cream; top each serving with guacamole mixture and desired toppings. Serve with lime wedges, if desired.

Cheese Substitution Note: Asadero is a mild Hispanic-style cheese that melts well. Monterey Jack is an excellent substitution.

Prep: 10 min. ✳ **Cook:** 24 min.

Curried Chicken with Basmati Rice

Makes 4 servings

The curry flavor in this dish is subtle and a nice introduction to Indian cuisine. "My three kids loved picking their own toppings. As a mom, I liked the fact that dinner was on the table in about 30 minutes." —Marianne D., Eldersburg, MD

MENU IDEA FOR 4

- Curried Chicken with Basmati Rice
- Sliced cucumbers
- Pita bread

GROCERIES NEEDED

Check staples: curry powder, vegetable oil, bottled minced garlic, soy sauce, ground red pepper, cornstarch, large eggs

- 1 1/2 lb. skinned and boned chicken breasts
- 1 red bell pepper
- 1 (13.5-oz.) can coconut milk
- 1 jar mango chutney
- 1 package basmati rice
- Accompaniments: 1 jar dry-roasted peanuts or cashews, 1 bunch green onions, 1 box raisins, 1 small can flaked coconut (optional)
- 2 cucumbers
- 2 (8-inch) pita bread rounds

PER ENTRÉE SERVING:
CALORIES 779 (39% from fat); FAT 33.8g (sat 19.8g, mono 5.9g, poly 5.3g); PROTEIN 46g; CARB 72.5g; FIBER 2.6g; CHOL 99mg; IRON 7.1mg; SODIUM 706mg; CALC 43mg

1 1/2 lb. skinned and boned chicken breasts, cut into 1-inch pieces
2 tsp. curry powder
3 Tbsp. vegetable oil, divided

1 red bell pepper, cut into strips
1 tsp. bottled minced garlic
1 (13.5-oz.) can coconut milk
1/2 cup mango chutney
1 tsp. soy sauce
1/8 tsp. ground red pepper

1 tsp. cornstarch
1 tsp. water
4 cups hot cooked basmati rice
Accompaniments: chopped dry-roasted peanuts or cashews, sliced green onion, chopped hard-cooked eggs, raisins, toasted coconut (optional)

1. Sprinkle chicken with curry powder. Heat 2 Tbsp. oil in a large skillet over medium-high heat until hot; add chicken, and sauté 5 minutes or until chicken is browned. Remove from pan.

2. Add remaining 1 Tbsp. oil to pan; heat over medium-high heat. Add bell pepper and garlic; sauté 2 to 3 minutes or until crisp-tender. Return chicken to pan; add coconut milk and next 3 ingredients. Bring to a boil; reduce heat, and simmer 12 minutes, stirring occasionally.

3. Combine cornstarch and water, stirring until smooth. Stir into chicken mixture. Bring to a boil over medium heat; boil, stirring constantly, 1 minute. Serve chicken mixture over basmati rice. Top with accompaniments, if desired.

Head-start Tip: While you're prepping this recipe, Marianne suggests cutting up twice as much chicken and red pepper and freezing them in plastic bags. Then you'll have a head start for the next time you prepare the recipe.

MENU IDEA FOR 4

- Gnocchi with Olive Oil, Tomato, and Parmesan
- Steamed asparagus
- Italian bread

GROCERIES NEEDED

Check staples: olive oil, bottled minced garlic, pepper, salt, shredded Parmesan cheese

- 1 (32-oz.) container chicken broth
- 1 (16-oz.) package vacuum-packed gnocchi (we tested with Ferrara)
- 1 bunch fresh sage (optional)
- 4 plum tomatoes
- 1 lb. fresh asparagus
- 1 loaf Italian bread

PER ENTRÉE SERVING:
CALORIES 309 (31% from fat); FAT 10.6g (sat 2.7g, mono 5.8g, poly 0.9g); PROTEIN 8.4g; CARB 45.2g; FIBER 2.3g; CHOL 8.4mg; IRON 1.2mg; SODIUM 909mg; CALC 133mg

Prep: 5 min. ✳ **Cook:** 14 min.

Gnocchi with Olive Oil, Tomato, and Parmesan

Makes 4 servings

"If I didn't know better I'd think my kids were Italian. They're crazy about sauce-laden dishes like lasagna and pizza. This recipe gave them a taste of the fresher side of Italian food. If we have sage in our herb garden, I use it. Otherwise, I just leave it out and it's just as good." —Lissy B., Boulder, CO

1 (32-oz.) container chicken broth
1 (16-oz.) package vacuum-packed gnocchi

2 Tbsp. olive oil
1 Tbsp. bottled minced garlic
10 to 12 fresh sage leaves (optional)

4 plum tomatoes, chopped
½ tsp. pepper
¼ tsp. salt
½ cup shredded Parmesan cheese

1. Place broth in a Dutch oven; add enough water to equal the amount necessary to cook gnocchi according to package directions. Prepare gnocchi as directed. Drain, reserving ¼ cup cooking liquid.

2. Heat oil in a small skillet over medium heat. Add garlic and sage, if desired; cook 2 to 3 minutes or until fragrant and sage leaves are crisp. Remove leaves, and drain on paper towels; set leaves aside. Reserve olive oil mixture in skillet.

3. In a large bowl, combine gnocchi, reserved garlic oil, reserved ¼ cup cooking liquid, tomato, pepper, and salt; toss to coat. Sprinkle with cheese and sage leaves.

Ingredient Note: Gnocchi (pronounced NYOH-kee) is a small dumpling made from potatoes, flour, and eggs. It's shelf-stable and cooks quickly. Chances are if your kids like pasta, they'll like this Italian specialty.

Kung Pao Chicken

Makes 4 servings

This is a tamer version of a traditional fiery Szechuan dish. Increase the ginger and red pepper if your family prefers heat, or eliminate them completely for a simple chicken and broccoli stir-fry.

1 Tbsp. canola or vegetable oil, divided
4 cups broccoli florets
1 tsp. bottled ground fresh ginger, divided
2 Tbsp. water

1 lb. skinned and boned chicken breasts, cut into ¼-inch strips
¼ tsp. dried crushed red pepper

½ cup chicken broth
2 Tbsp. rice wine vinegar
2 Tbsp. soy sauce
2 Tbsp. hoisin sauce
2 tsp. bottled minced garlic
1 tsp. cornstarch
2 Tbsp. coarsely chopped salted peanuts

1. Heat 1 tsp. oil in a large nonstick skillet over medium-high heat. Add broccoli and ½ tsp. ginger to pan; sauté 1 minute. Add 2 Tbsp. water. Cover and cook 2 minutes or until broccoli is crisp-tender. Remove broccoli from pan; keep warm.

2. Heat remaining 2 tsp. oil in pan; add remaining ½ tsp. ginger, chicken, and crushed red pepper. Cook 4 minutes or until chicken is lightly browned, stirring often.

3. Whisk together broth and next 5 ingredients in a small bowl. Add broth mixture to pan; cook 1 minute or until mixture thickens, stirring constantly. Return broccoli mixture to pan; toss to coat. Sprinkle with peanuts.

Table Talk: In Asian cultures, most children eat with chopsticks by the age of three. Just as we have small forks and spoons designed for toddlers, chopsticks come in training varieties, too. They're shorter and often hinged to keep them in line.

MENU IDEA FOR 4
- Kung Pao Chicken
- Rice
- Cucumber-tomato salad

GROCERIES NEEDED

Check staples: canola or vegetable oil, bottled ground fresh ginger, dried crushed red pepper, soy sauce, hoisin sauce, bottled minced garlic, cornstarch, salad dressing
- 3 broccoli crowns
- 1 lb. skinned and boned chicken breasts
- 1 (14-oz.) can chicken broth
- 1 small bottle rice wine vinegar
- 1 jar salted peanuts
- 1 package rice
- 2 tomatoes
- 2 cucumbers

PER ENTRÉE SERVING:
CALORIES 248 (31% from fat); FAT 8.6g (sat 1.4g, mono 2.5g, poly 1.6g); PROTEIN 31g; CARB 9.6g; FIBER 2.7g; CHOL 67mg; IRON 1.6mg; SODIUM 913mg; CALC 50mg

Prep: 5 min. ☀ **Cook:** 8 min.

Beef Fillets with Blue Cheese Butter

Makes 4 servings

This recipe and the following nine recipes are all about options to suit every member of the family. You'll serve part of each recipe plain and simple while the rest is embellished for the grown-ups with more adult-friendly ingredients. In this case, a simple tenderloin fillet is served unadorned for the youngsters and topped with a sophisticated Blue Cheese Butter for the grown-ups.

MENU IDEA FOR 4

- Beef Fillets with Blue Cheese Butter
- Steamed asparagus
- Crusty French rolls

GROCERIES NEEDED

Check staples: salt, pepper, butter, olive oil cooking spray

- 4 (4-oz.) beef tenderloin fillets (about 1 inch thick)
- 1 (4-oz.) package crumbled blue cheese
- 1 bunch fresh chives or 1 container frozen chopped chives
- 1 lb. fresh asparagus
- Crusty French rolls

PER GROWN-UP ENTRÉE SERVING:
CALORIES 327 (70% from fat);
FAT 25.6g (sat 11.5g, mono 10.1g, poly 1g); PROTEIN 22.7g;
CARB 0.2g; FIBER 0.1g;
CHOL 88mg; IRON 1.7mg;
SODIUM 403mg; CALC 38mg

PER PLAIN ENTRÉE SERVING:
CALORIES 281 (66% from fat);
FAT 20.6g (sat 8.3g, mono 8.8g, poly 0.8g); PROTEIN 22.3g;
CARB 0.2g; FIBER 0.1g; CHOL 75mg;
IRON 1.7mg; SODIUM 348mg;
CALC 27mg

4 (4-oz.) beef tenderloin fillets (about 1 inch thick)
½ tsp. salt
½ tsp. pepper

½ cup butter, softened
¼ cup crumbled blue cheese
2 Tbsp. chopped fresh or frozen chives

Olive oil cooking spray

1. Sprinkle fillets evenly with salt and pepper. Let stand at room temperature.

2. Meanwhile, combine butter, blue cheese, and chives a small bowl; stir using a wooden spoon until blended. Cover and chill.

3. Place a large nonstick skillet over medium-high heat until hot. Pat fillets dry with paper towels, and coat both sides with cooking spray. Add fillets to pan; cook 3 to 4 minutes on each side or until desired degree of doneness. For grown-up servings, top 2 fillets with 1 Tbsp. each of Blue Cheese Butter. For plain servings, serve fillets without Blue Cheese Butter.

Leftover Note: Christine H., of Danville, CA, suggests spooning the leftover Blue Cheese Butter into 1 Tbsp. portions in a single layer on a large plate. Freeze until firm; then transfer to an airtight container, and freeze up to 1 month. Use the butter again to prepare this recipe or to season your favorite steamed vegetables.

GROCERIES NEEDED

Check staples: bottled minced garlic, dried crushed red pepper, dried basil, shredded Parmesan cheese

- 1 (8-oz.) package spaghetti
- 32 Italian-style frozen, precooked meatballs
- 1 (26-oz.) jar fire-roasted tomato garlic pasta sauce (we tested with Classico)
- 1 small jar kalamata olives
- 1 small jar capers
- 1 tube anchovy paste
- 1 lemon
- 1 (15-oz.) package complete Caesar salad kit

PER GROWN-UP ENTRÉE SERVING:
CALORIES 725 (46% from fat);
FAT 36.9g (sat 12.6g, mono 2.1g, poly 0.9g); PROTEIN 34.5g;
CARB 69g; FIBER 12.1g;
CHOL 73mg; IRON 6mg;
SODIUM 2549mg; CALC 212mg

PER PLAIN ENTRÉE SERVING:
CALORIES 616 (48% from fat);
FAT 32.6g (sat 12.1g, mono 0.1g, poly 0.4g); PROTEIN 30g;
CARB 57.3g; FIBER 9.7g;
CHOL 67mg; IRON 4.6mg;
SODIUM 1620mg; CALC 124mg

Prep: 5 min. ❋ **Cook:** 12 min.

Spaghetti and Meatballs Puttanesca

Makes 4 servings

"This basic kids' recipe uses meatballs, a simple jarred marinara, and pasta, and I find that a little boring. Adding a few robust ingredients like capers, anchovy paste, and crushed red pepper to my portion makes me feel like I'm eating from the adult menu."—Lynda M., Aurora, IL

8 oz. spaghetti, uncooked

32 Italian-style frozen, precooked meatballs, divided
1 (26-oz.) jar fire-roasted tomato garlic pasta sauce, divided
2 Tbsp. coarsely chopped kalamata olives
1 Tbsp. capers
2 tsp. anchovy paste
1 tsp. bottled minced garlic
½ tsp. dried crushed red pepper
½ tsp. dried basil
1 lemon wedge, seeded

Shredded Parmesan cheese (optional)

1. Cook spaghetti according to package directions; drain.

2. Meanwhile, combine half the meatballs, two-thirds of the pasta sauce, and next 6 ingredients in a medium saucepan. Squeeze juice from lemon wedge into sauce; bring to a boil. Reduce heat, and simmer 10 minutes, stirring occasionally.

3. Combine remaining meatballs and pasta sauce in a glass bowl. Cover with plastic wrap; fold back a small edge to allow steam to escape. Microwave at HIGH 1½ minutes or until hot.

4. To serve, divide spaghetti evenly among 4 serving plates. For plain servings, spoon microwaved sauce over 2 portions. For grown-up servings, spoon seasoned sauce over remaining 2 portions. Sprinkle all 4 portions with Parmesan cheese, if desired.

Shopping Note: Anchovy paste is typically located near canned tuna and anchovies. After opening, store it in the refrigerator up to 6 months.

MENU IDEA FOR 5

- Honey Brats with Sweet-and-Spicy Slaw
- Potato chips

GROCERIES NEEDED

Check staples: caraway seeds, honey, vegetable cooking spray, ketchup, mustard

- 1 (19.76-oz.) package bratwurst (we tested with Johnsonville)
- 1 large onion
- 1 (10-oz.) package shredded angel hair coleslaw mix
- 2 cups apple cider
- 1 bottle Thousand Island dressing
- 1 small jar deli mustard with grated horseradish
- 5 whole wheat or white pita rollups or hot dog buns
- Potato chips

PER GROWN-UP ENTRÉE SERVING:
CALORIES 542 (59% from fat);
FAT 35.7g (sat 10.8g, mono 3.3g,
poly 4.4g); PROTEIN 18.8g;
CARB 35.2g; FIBER 3.2g;
CHOL 71mg; IRON 2.5mg;
SODIUM 1284mg; CALC 66mg

PER PLAIN ENTRÉE SERVING:
CALORIES 434 (58% from fat);
FAT 28.1g (sat 9.8g, mono 1.6g,
poly 0.5g); PROTEIN 17.6g;
CARB 25.6g; FIBER 1.3g;
CHOL 65mg; IRON 2.1mg;
SODIUM 1089mg; CALC 51mg

Prep: 8 min. ❋ Cook: 26 min.

Honey Brats with Sweet-and-Spicy Slaw

Makes 5 servings

The younger ones may prefer a no-frills brat with just ketchup and mustard. Add the slaw for those who want theirs dressed all the way.

1 (19.76-oz.) package bratwurst
1 large onion, halved and thinly sliced
1 (10-oz.) package shredded angel hair coleslaw mix
2 tsp. caraway seeds
2 cups apple cider

½ cup Thousand Island dressing

2 Tbsp. deli mustard with grated horseradish
1 Tbsp. honey
Vegetable cooking spray
5 whole wheat or white pita rollups or hot dog buns

1. Pierce each brat with a fork, and place in a large saucepan. Top with onion and coleslaw mix; sprinkle with caraway seeds. Pour apple cider over cabbage mixture; bring to a boil. Cover, reduce heat to medium, and cook 20 minutes or until cabbage is tender. Remove brats, and set aside.

2. Drain cabbage mixture well, reserving 2 Tbsp. cooking liquid. Discard remaining cooking liquid. Combine cabbage mixture, reserved cooking liquid, and Thousand Island dressing in a large bowl; toss to coat. Cover and chill.

3. Combine mustard and honey in a small bowl; set aside. Place a large nonstick skillet coated with cooking spray over medium-high heat until hot. Add brats to pan; cook about 6 minutes or until golden brown on all sides, turning often and basting with honey mixture. For grown-up servings, place 1 brat in a pita rollup with ⅓ cup slaw. For plain servings, serve brats in pita rollups without the slaw.

Prep: 14 min. ✳ Cook: 20 min.

Crisp Orange Roughy with Tropical Salsa

Makes 4 servings

Jan P., of Ponte Vedra Beach, FL, thought her son would like the plain serving of fish with just a crispy cornflake coating. And he did. A simple tropical salsa dressed it up for the more trendy expectations of the parents.

½ cup coarsely chopped fresh pineapple
½ cup coarsely chopped fresh mango
2 Tbsp. chopped green onions
1 Tbsp. light brown sugar
1 Tbsp. fresh lime juice
1 Tbsp. olive oil
¼ tsp. salt
⅛ tsp. dried crushed red pepper

2 Tbsp. mayonnaise
1 Tbsp. Dijon mustard
4 (6-oz.) orange roughy or other white fish fillets
2 cups cornflakes cereal, coarsely crushed (1 cup crushed)

1. Combine first 8 ingredients in a medium bowl; cover salsa, and chill.

2. Preheat oven to 400°. Combine mayonnaise and mustard in a small bowl; brush evenly over both sides of each fish fillet. Coat fillets with crushed cereal.

3. Heat a well-greased jellyroll pan in oven 5 minutes. Remove pan from oven; place fish several inches apart on hot pan. Bake at 400° for 15 minutes or until fish flakes with a fork. For grown-up servings, top each fish fillet with ¼ cup salsa. For plain servings, serve fillets without salsa.

MENU IDEA FOR 4

- Crisp Orange Roughy with Tropical Salsa
- Steamed snow peas

GROCERIES NEEDED

Check staples: light brown sugar, olive oil, salt, dried crushed red pepper, mayonnaise, Dijon mustard

- 1 peeled and cored fresh pineapple
- 1 fresh mango
- 1 bunch green onions
- 1 lime
- 4 (6-oz.) orange roughy or other white fish fillets
- 1 box cornflakes cereal
- 1 lb. fresh snow peas or 2 (6-oz.) packages frozen snow peas

PER GROWN-UP ENTRÉE SERVING: CALORIES 276 (33% from fat); FAT 10.2g (sat 1.3g, mono 2.9g, poly 0.6g); PROTEIN 28.8g; CARB 16.8g; FIBER 1g; CHOL 105mg; IRON 4.6mg; SODIUM 431mg; CALC 25mg

PER PLAIN ENTRÉE SERVING: CALORIES 213 (29% from fat); FAT 6.8g (sat 0.8g, mono 0.4g, poly 0.2g); PROTEIN 28.5g; CARB 8.1g; FIBER 0.2g; CHOL 105mg; IRON 4.4mg; SODIUM 283mg; CALC 16mg

MENU IDEA FOR 4

- Egg Noodles in Cream Sauce with Asiago
- Spinach salad

GROCERIES NEEDED

Check staples: chicken bouillon granules, salt, olive oil, grated Parmesan cheese, white pepper, salad dressing

- 1 (8-oz.) package wide egg noodles
- 1 qt. whipping cream
- 1 bottle dry white wine or 1 (14-oz.) can chicken broth
- 4 oz. shiitake mushrooms
- 1 package frozen sweet peas
- ¹/₂ cup grated Asiago cheese
- 1 (12-oz.) package fresh spinach

PER GROWN-UP ENTRÉE SERVING:
CALORIES 976 (68% from fat); FAT 73.8g (sat 37.3g, mono 27.6g, poly 2.5g); PROTEIN 17.6g; CARB 56.8g; FIBER 4.6g; CHOL 265mg; IRON 3.8mg; SODIUM 915mg; CALC 390mg

PER PLAIN ENTRÉE SERVING:
CALORIES 703 (69% from fat); FAT 53.6g (sat 31g, mono 16g, poly 0.8g); PROTEIN 7.3g; CARB 45.3g; FIBER 1.7g; CHOL 242mg; IRON 2.1mg; SODIUM 794mg; CALC 146mg

Prep: 8 min. ❄ **Cook:** 15 min.

Egg Noodles in Cream Sauce with Asiago

Makes 4 servings

These noodles are divided just before serving: two servings are left plain for picky palates, while the others are daringly dressed with shiitake mushrooms and Asiago cheese.

3 qt. water
1 Tbsp. chicken bouillon granules
1 (8-oz.) package wide egg noodles

2½ cups whipping cream
¼ cup dry white wine or chicken broth
½ tsp. salt

4 oz. sliced shiitake mushrooms
¾ cup frozen sweet peas
2 Tbsp. olive oil

1 Tbsp. grated Parmesan cheese
½ cup grated Asiago cheese
¼ tsp. ground white pepper

1. Combine water and chicken bouillon granules in a Dutch oven; bring to a boil. Add noodles, and cook according to package directions. Drain and return to Dutch oven.

2. Meanwhile, combine whipping cream, wine, and salt in a large saucepan; cook over medium-high heat 5 minutes or until reduced to 2 cups.

3. Sauté mushrooms and peas in hot olive oil in a large skillet over medium-high heat 5 minutes or until mushrooms are tender.

4. Pour cream mixture over noodles; toss to coat. To serve, divide noodle mixture evenly among 4 serving plates. For plain servings, top 2 portions with Parmesan cheese. For grown-up servings, top remaining 2 portions with mushroom mixture, Asiago cheese, and white pepper. Stir gently to blend.

MENU IDEA FOR 4

- Have-It-Your-Way Pizza
- BLT Caesar salad

GROCERIES NEEDED

Check staples: olive oil

- 1 (24-oz.) package refrigerated pizza crusts (we tested with Mama Mary's)
- 2 plum tomatoes
- 8 kalamata olives
- 1 small red onion
- 1 jar pizza sauce (we tested with Ragú)
- 2 oz. crumbled feta cheese with basil and sun-dried tomato
- 1 cup (4 oz.) shred-ded Cheddar-mozzarella cheese blend
- 1 (8-oz.) package complete BLT Caesar salad kit (such as Fresh Express)

PER GROWN-UP ENTRÉE SERVING:
CALORIES 405 (39% from fat);
FAT 17.4g (sat 5.2g, mono 4.7g,
poly 0.8g); PROTEIN 14g;
CARB 49.2g; FIBER 3.6g;
CHOL 21mg; IRON 2.8mg;
SODIUM 1222mg; CALC 113mg

PER PLAIN ENTRÉE SERVING:
CALORIES 445 (38% from fat);
FAT 18.6g (sat 8.9g, mono 1.6g,
poly 0.2g); PROTEIN 22.1g;
CARB 44.8g; FIBER 2.6g;
CHOL 40mg; IRON 2.5mg;
SODIUM 1037mg; CALC 500mg

Prep: 12 min. ❋ **Cook:** 13 min.

Have-It-Your-Way Pizza

Makes 4 servings

Here's a pizza that delivers just what the kids want on half the crust—a thin layer of pizza sauce and lots of gooey cheese. There are lots of extras on the other side for more adventurous palates.

2 tsp. olive oil
½ (24-oz.) package refrigerated pizza crusts

2 plum tomatoes
8 pitted kalamata or other ripe olives
¼ small red onion

⅔ cup pizza sauce
2 oz. crumbled feta cheese with basil and sun-dried tomato
1 cup (4 oz.) shredded Cheddar-mozzarella cheese blend

1. Preheat oven to 425°. Brush oil over pizza crust; place on an ungreased baking sheet. Bake at 425° for 5 minutes.

2. Meanwhile, thinly slice tomatoes, halve olives, and thinly slice onion.

3. Remove crust from oven; spread pizza sauce over pizza crust, leaving a 1-inch margin. Arrange tomato, olives, and onion over half of pizza; sprinkle with feta cheese. Sprinkle Cheddar-mozzarella cheese over remaining half of pizza.

4. Bake at 425° for 8 minutes or just until cheese melts.

Prep: 13 min. ❋ **Cook:** 23 min.

Hot-or-Not Skillet Chops

Makes 6 servings

If the grown-ups like spicy foods while the kids
prefer less heat, try this recipe. Serve 2 chops plain,
and coat the others with the sweet, spicy glaze.

GROCERIES NEEDED

Check staples: garlic
salt, pepper, all-purpose
flour, vegetable oil,
honey, butter

• 1 (7-oz.) can chipotle
  peppers in adobo
  sauce

• 6 ($^1/_2$-inch-thick)
  boneless pork chops
  (about 1$^1/_2$ lb.)

• 1 medium onion

• 1 (14-oz.) can chicken
  broth

• 1 package basmati
  rice

• 6 red plums

PER GROWN-UP ENTRÉE SERVING:
CALORIES 296 (45% from fat);
FAT 14.7g (sat 4.5g, mono 6.7g,
poly 2g); PROTEIN 25.4g;
CARB 15.1g; FIBER 0.6g;
CHOL 71mg; IRON 1.1mg;
SODIUM 1,175mg; CALC 40mg

PER PLAIN ENTRÉE SERVING:
CALORIES 239 (51% from fat);
FAT 13.5g (sat 4.3g, mono 6g,
poly 1.9g); PROTEIN 24.8g;
CARB 3g; FIBER 0.1g; CHOL 70mg;
IRON 0.9mg; SODIUM 209mg;
CALC 29mg

1 (7-oz.) can chipotle peppers in
  adobo sauce

6 ($^1/_2$-inch-thick) boneless pork chops
  (about 1$^1/_2$ lb.)
1 tsp. garlic salt
$^1/_4$ tsp. pepper
$^1/_3$ cup all-purpose flour
3 Tbsp. vegetable oil, divided

1$^1/_2$ cups vertically sliced onion
  1 cup chicken broth, divided
$^1/_4$ cup honey

1. Remove 1 pepper from can; finely
chop, and set aside. Measure 2 Tbsp.
sauce from can; set aside. Reserve remaining
peppers and sauce for other uses.

2. Sprinkle chops with garlic salt and pepper;
dredge in flour, shaking off excess.
Heat 1 Tbsp. oil in a large skillet over
medium-high heat; add 3 chops, and cook
2 minutes on each side or until browned.
Remove from pan; keep warm. Repeat
with 1 Tbsp. oil and remaining chops.

3. Heat remaining 1 Tbsp. oil in pan;
sauté onion in hot oil until lightly
browned. Add $^1/_2$ cup broth, stirring to
loosen browned bits from pan; cook 2
minutes. Return chops to pan; bring to a
boil. Cover, reduce heat, and simmer 5
minutes or until done. Remove chops;
keep warm.

4. Add chopped chipotle pepper, adobo
sauce, remaining $^1/_2$ cup broth, and honey
to pan. Bring to a boil; cook 5 minutes or
until thickened. For grown-up servings,
spoon 2 Tbsp. chipotle mixture over 2
chops. For plain servings, serve chops
without chipotle mixture.

258

Prep: 30 min. ✳ **Cook:** 10 min.

Stuffed Tex-Mex Burgers

Makes 6 servings

The kiddos will devour these cheese-filled burgers with the condiments of their choice, while the adults can dress them with an added kick from the jalapeño mayonnaise and guacamole.

½ cup mayonnaise
2 Tbsp. chopped fresh cilantro
1 Tbsp. fresh lime juice
½ jalapeño pepper, seeded and finely minced
⅛ tsp. pepper

1½ lb. ground chuck
2 Tbsp. grated onion
½ tsp. salt
6 (.8-oz.) slices Cheddar cheese

6 (1.5-oz.) hamburger buns, split and toasted
1 (8-oz.) package refrigerated guacamole
Toppings: shredded lettuce, tomato slices (optional)

1. Process first 5 ingredients in a food processor or blender until smooth; chill.

2. Preheat grill to medium-high (350° to 400°). Combine ground chuck, onion, and salt; shape into 12 (4-inch) patties. Fold cheese slices into quarters; top 6 patties with a folded cheese slice. Cover cheese with remaining 6 patties, pressing to seal edges.

3. Grill patties, covered with grill lid, over medium-high heat 5 minutes on each side or until done. For grown-up servings, serve burgers on buns with 2 Tbsp. guacamole, 1 Tbsp. mayonnaise mixture, and desired toppings. For plain servings, serve burgers on buns without guacamole and mayonnaise mixture.

Preparation Note: Romana F., from Laytonsville, MD, makes uniform hamburger patties quickly with a biscuit or cookie cutter. For this recipe, she divides the meat mixture into 12 equal portions on a piece of wax paper or aluminum foil. She then places each portion of meat into the cutter and presses it into a patty. Her kids like to join in on the patty making, too.

MENU IDEA FOR 6
• Stuffed Tex-Mex Burgers
• Tortilla chips with salsa or bean dip

GROCERIES NEEDED

Check staples: mayonnaise, pepper, salt
• 1 bunch fresh cilantro
• 1 lime
• 1 jalapeño pepper
• 1½ lb. ground chuck
• 1 small onion
• 6 (.8-oz.) slices Cheddar cheese
• 6 (1.5-oz.) hamburger buns
• 1 (8-oz.) package refrigerated guacamole (we tested with Avo Classic)
• 1 head leaf lettuce
• 1 medium tomato
• 1 bag tortilla chips
• 1 jar salsa or bean dip

PER GROWN-UP ENTRÉE SERVING:
CALORIES 629 (65% from fat); FAT 45.6g (sat 16g, mono 12.5g, poly 1.7g); PROTEIN 29.7g; CARB 23.5g; FIBER 2g; CHOL 109mg; IRON 3.9mg; SODIUM 776mg; CALC 249mg

PER PLAIN ENTRÉE SERVING:
CALORIES 499 (58% from fat); FAT 32g (sat 14g, mono 12.5g, poly 1.6g); PROTEIN 29.2g; CARB 21.7g; FIBER 0.9g; CHOL 104mg; IRON 3.8mg; SODIUM 612mg; CALC 243mg

MENU IDEA FOR 4

- Chicken Alfredo with Dried Tomatoes and Spinach

- Italian bread

GROCERIES NEEDED

Check staples: milk, butter, pepper, ground nutmeg (optional)

- 8 oz. uncooked fettuccine

- 1 (1.6-oz.) package Alfredo sauce mix (we tested with Knorr)

- 2 (6-oz.) packages refrigerated grilled chicken breast strips (we tested with Tyson)

- 1 small wedge Parmesan cheese

- 1 small bag fresh baby spinach

- 1 small jar oil-packed dried tomatoes

- Italian bread

PER GROWN-UP ENTRÉE SERVING:
CALORIES 515 (29% from fat); FAT 16.5g (sat 7.1g, mono 3.7g, poly 0.8g); PROTEIN 35.3g; CARB 58g; FIBER 3.2g; CHOL 81mg; IRON 3.4mg; SODIUM 1811mg; CALC 222mg

PER PLAIN ENTRÉE SERVING:
CALORIES 474 (26% from fat); FAT 13.9g (sat 6.7g, mono 2.1g, poly 0.4g); PROTEIN 34.2g; CARB 53g; FIBER 1.8g; CHOL 81mg; IRON 2.7mg; SODIUM 1752mg; CALC 209mg

Prep: 15 min. ❄ **Cook:** 20 min.

Chicken Alfredo with Dried Tomatoes and Spinach

Makes 4 servings

"I liked this recipe because it was easy, the kids liked their simple portions, and ours was jazzed up with spinach and dried tomatoes." —Sarah V., Cypress, TX

8 oz. uncooked fettuccine

1 (1.6-oz.) package Alfredo sauce mix
1½ cups milk
1 Tbsp. butter or margarine
¼ tsp. pepper
⅛ tsp. ground nutmeg (optional)
2 (6-oz.) packages refrigerated grilled chicken breast strips

1 oz. piece Parmesan cheese, shaved
½ cup thinly sliced fresh baby spinach
⅓ cup oil-packed dried tomatoes, thinly sliced

1. Cook fettuccine according to package directions; drain.

2. Meanwhile, whisk together Alfredo sauce mix and milk in a large saucepan; add butter. Bring to a boil over medium-high heat, whisking often. Reduce heat, and simmer 2 minutes. Stir in pepper and nutmeg, if desired. Combine sauce, chicken strips, and hot cooked pasta in a large bowl; toss well.

3. For plain servings, spoon half of pasta mixture evenly onto 2 serving plates; top with half of Parmesan cheese. For grown-up servings, add spinach and dried tomatoes to remaining pasta mixture; stir gently to blend. Spoon evenly onto 2 serving plates, and top with remaining Parmesan cheese.

Prep: 13 min. ✳ **Cook:** 10 min. ✳ **Other:** 1 hr.

Grilled Mahi Mahi with Avocado Butter

Makes 4 servings

Kids think this fish tastes great all by itself, and grown-ups love it slathered with the Avocado Butter. You might want to try expanding the kids' taste buds and top their fish with a small amount of Avocado Butter. Jenn D., of Firestone, CO, tried it and her 5-year-old loved it!

MENU IDEA FOR 4

- Grilled Mahi Mahi with Avocado Butter
- Grilled cherry tomato kabobs

GROCERIES NEEDED

Check staples: olive oil, soy sauce, bottled minced garlic, butter, salt, ground red pepper, wooden skewers

- 4 (6-oz.) mahi mahi fillets
- 4 limes
- 1 ripe avocado
- 1 bunch fresh cilantro
- 1 pt. cherry tomatoes

PER GROWN-UP ENTRÉE SERVING:
CALORIES 230 (40% from fat); FAT 10.1g (sat 3.8g, mono 4.4g, poly 0.9g); PROTEIN 32.2g; CARB 1.1g; FIBER 0.3g; CHOL 136mg; IRON 2mg; SODIUM 471mg; CALC 29mg

PER PLAIN ENTRÉE SERVING:
CALORIES 180 (23% from fat); FAT 4.6g (sat 0.8g, mono 2.7g, poly 0.6g); PROTEIN 32g; CARB 0.6g; FIBER 0g; CHOL 124mg; IRON 2mg; SODIUM 380mg; CALC 27mg

4 (6-oz.) mahi mahi fillets
2 Tbsp. olive oil
2 Tbsp. soy sauce
½ tsp. grated lime rind
¼ cup fresh lime juice, divided
1 tsp. bottled minced garlic, divided

¼ cup butter, softened
¼ cup mashed ripe avocado
1 Tbsp. chopped fresh cilantro
¼ tsp. salt
⅛ tsp. ground red pepper
Garnish: lime wedges

1. Place fillets in a large zip-top freezer bag; add oil, soy sauce, lime rind, 3 Tbsp. lime juice, and ½ tsp. garlic. Seal and chill 1 hour, turning occasionally.

2. Preheat grill to medium-high (350° to 400°). Whisk together butter, avocado, cilantro, remaining 1 Tbsp. fresh lime juice, remaining ½ tsp garlic, salt, and red pepper until well blended.

3. Remove fish from marinade, discarding marinade. Grill fish, covered with grill lid, over medium-high heat 4 to 5 minutes on each side or until fish flakes with a fork. For grown-up servings, spoon 1 Tbsp. Avocado Butter over 2 fish fillets. For plain servings, serve remaining 2 fillets without Avocado Butter. Garnish, if desired.

Leftover Note: Use remaining Avocado Butter on other entrées and vegetables.

Side Dish Note: Cherry tomato kabobs are quick, nutritious, and add color to the plate. Soak wooden skewers in water 30 minutes, and drain. Thread cherry tomatoes onto skewers, and grill alongside fish about 6 minutes or until barely charred and hot, turning frequently.

Prep: 16 min. ❋ **Cook:** 12 min.

Pecan Chicken with Cream Sauce

Makes 4 servings

You'd be surprised how many kids have sophisticated taste buds. This recipe and those that follow get high fives from our own adventurous young taste testers. They loved the nutty crunch and rich cream sauce in this recipe.

³/₄ cup pecan halves
½ cup fine, dry breadcrumbs

4 (6-oz.) skinned and boned chicken breasts
¼ tsp. salt
¼ tsp. pepper
2 Tbsp. butter or margarine, melted
2 Tbsp. Dijon mustard, divided

3 Tbsp. vegetable oil
¼ cup whipping cream
¼ cup chicken broth

1. Process pecans in a food processor or blender until finely ground. Combine ground pecans and breadcrumbs in a shallow dish; set aside.

2. Sprinkle chicken with salt and pepper. Stir together butter and 1 Tbsp. mustard in a bowl. Brush each chicken breast with mustard mixture; dredge in pecan mixture.

3. Heat oil in a large skillet over medium heat until hot; cook chicken 4 minutes on each side or until done. Remove chicken from pan; keep warm. Add whipping cream, broth, and remaining 1 Tbsp. mustard to drippings in pan; cook 4 minutes, stirring constantly, until sauce thickens. Serve sauce over chicken.

Equipment Tip: A mini-food processor is just the right size to grind the small amount of pecans in step 1.

GROCERIES NEEDED

Check staples: butter, dried thyme, salt, pepper

- 1 medium butternut squash (about 2 lb.)

- 1 medium leek or large sweet onion

- 2 (14-oz.) cans chicken broth

- 3 fully cooked bacon slices

- 1 (8-oz.) container sour cream

- 1 bunch fresh thyme (optional)

- 1 loaf sandwich bread

- 1 package Cheddar cheese slices

- 6 medium pears

PER 1¹/₂ CUPS SOUP:
CALORIES 173 (50% from fat); FAT 9.6g (sat 4.9g, mono 1.8g, poly 0.3g); PROTEIN 4.5g; CARB 18.4g; FIBER 2.9g; CHOL 28mg; IRON 1.3mg; SODIUM 1076mg; CALCIUM 79mg

Prep: 15 min. ✳ **Cook:** 50 min.

Hearty Butternut Squash and Bacon Soup

Makes 9 cups

"My entire family loves butternut squash. It has a sweet, buttery flavor and thickens soup similar to potatoes. As you might guess by its deep-orange color, it's a great source of beta-carotene." —Kathy C., San Marcos, CA

1 medium butternut squash (about 2 lb.)

3 Tbsp. butter or margarine
1 medium leek or large sweet onion, sliced
¹/₂ tsp. dried thyme
2 (14-oz.) cans chicken broth

¹/₄ tsp. salt
¹/₄ tsp. pepper
Toppings: crumbled bacon, sour cream
Garnish: fresh thyme

1. Cut squash in half lengthwise; discard seeds. Place squash, cut sides down, in a microwave-safe dish. Microwave at HIGH 7 to 10 minutes or until tender; cool. Scoop out pulp, discarding shells.

2. Melt butter in a large Dutch oven over medium heat; add leek and thyme. Cook, stirring occasionally, 15 minutes or until caramel-colored and tender. Add squash pulp and chicken broth; bring to a boil. Reduce heat, and simmer 10 minutes, stirring often. Remove from heat; cool.

3. Process squash mixture in a blender until smooth, stopping to scrape down sides. Return to Dutch oven; stir in salt and pepper. Cook 5 minutes or until thoroughly heated. Serve with bacon and sour cream. Garnish, if desired.

Squash Note: Here's a simple way to halve a butternut squash. Make a shallow lengthwise cut in the skin with a sharp knife. Place the blade of a chef's knife in the shallow cut and tap the knife blade with a mallet until the squash is cut through.

MENU IDEA FOR 8

- Three-Cheese Chicken Penne
- Sliced tomatoes

GROCERIES NEEDED

Check staples: olive oil, vegetable cooking spray, pepper, grated Parmesan cheese, milk

- 8 oz. penne or other tube-shaped pasta
- 1 (8-oz.) package sliced fresh mushrooms
- 1 small onion
- 1 small red bell pepper
- 1 (6-oz.) package fresh spinach
- 1 Tbsp. chopped fresh oregano or 1 tsp. dried oregano
- 1 (16-oz.) container cottage cheese
- 1 rotisserie chicken
- 1 cup (4 oz.) shredded sharp Cheddar cheese
- 1 (10³/₄-oz.) can cream of chicken soup
- 4 tomatoes

PER ENTRÉE SERVING:
CALORIES 356 (34% from fat);
FAT 13.4g (sat 6.8g, mono 2.7g, poly 0.6g); PROTEIN 29.4g;
CARB 30.5g; FIBER 2.1g;
CHOL 61mg; IRON 2mg;
SODIUM 824mg; CALC 252mg

Prep: 20 min. ❋ **Cook:** 32 min.

Three-Cheese Chicken Penne

Makes 8 servings

Most kids won't even blink at the sight of spinach when it's smothered in a cheesy sauce. You'll be happy to know this is markedly lower in fat than a traditional pasta and cheese dish.

8 oz. penne (tube-shaped pasta), uncooked

1 tsp. olive oil
Vegetable cooking spray
1 (8-oz.) package sliced fresh mushrooms
1 small onion, chopped
1 small red bell pepper, chopped
3 cups chopped fresh spinach
1 Tbsp. chopped fresh oregano or 1 tsp. dried oregano
¼ tsp. pepper

1 (16-oz.) container cottage cheese
2 cups shredded roasted chicken
1 cup (4 oz.) shredded sharp Cheddar cheese, divided
½ cup grated Parmesan cheese, divided
½ cup milk
1 (10³/₄-oz.) can cream of chicken soup, undiluted

1. Cook pasta according to package directions; drain.

2. Preheat oven to 425°. Heat olive oil in a large skillet coated with cooking spray over medium-high heat until hot. Add mushrooms, onion, and bell pepper; sauté 4 minutes or until tender. Add spinach, oregano, and pepper; sauté 3 minutes or just until spinach wilts. Set aside.

3. Place cottage cheese in a food processor; process until very smooth. Combine cottage cheese, spinach mixture, cooked pasta, chicken, ¾ cup Cheddar cheese, ¼ cup Parmesan cheese, milk, and soup in a large bowl; stir until well blended. Spoon mixture into a 2-qt. baking dish coated with cooking spray. Sprinkle with remaining Cheddar and Parmesan cheeses. Bake at 425° for 25 minutes or until lightly browned and bubbly.

Container Note: Bake the pasta mixture in eight 8-oz. ramekins, if desired; bake for only 15 minutes.

MENU IDEA FOR 4

- Sautéed Tilapia with Lemon-Peppercorn Sauce
- Rice
- Creamed spinach

GROCERIES NEEDED

Check staples: butter, vegetable oil, salt, pepper, all-purpose flour

- 1 (14-oz.) can chicken broth
- 4 lemons
- 1 jar brine-packed green peppercorns
- 4 (6-oz.) tilapia or sole fillets
- 1 (16-oz.) package rice
- 1 (10-oz.) package frozen creamed spinach

PER ENTRÉE SERVING:
CALORIES 301 (35% from fat); FAT 11.8g (sat 4.8g, mono 3.3g, poly 1.9g); PROTEIN 36.4g; CARB 12.7g; FIBER 0.7g; CHOL 104mg; IRON 1.6mg; SODIUM 1100mg; CALC 30mg

Prep: 10 min. ❋ **Cook:** 12 min.

Sautéed Tilapia with Lemon-Peppercorn Sauce

Makes 4 servings

This piquant sauce is perfect over a mild white fish. The freshly squeezed lemon juice brings out the brightest flavor.

1½ cups chicken broth
½ cup fresh lemon juice
1 Tbsp. drained brine-packed green peppercorns, lightly crushed

6 tsp. butter or margarine, divided
2 tsp. vegetable oil
4 (6-oz.) tilapia or sole fillets
½ tsp. salt
½ tsp. pepper
½ cup all-purpose flour

Lemon wedges (optional)

1. Combine first 3 ingredients; set aside.

2. Melt 2 tsp. butter with oil in a large skillet over low heat. While butter melts, sprinkle fish fillets with salt and pepper. Place flour in a shallow dish. Dredge fillets in flour, shaking off excess flour.

3. Increase heat to medium-high; cook the butter and oil mixture 2 minutes or until butter turns golden brown. Add fillets to pan; cook 3 minutes on each side or until fish flakes with a fork. Remove fillets from pan.

4. Add broth mixture to pan, scraping to loosen browned bits. Bring to a boil; cook until reduced to about ½ cup. Remove from heat. Stir in remaining 4 tsp. butter with a whisk. Spoon sauce over fillets. Serve with lemon wedges, if desired.

Ingredient Note: Brine-packed green peppercorns are soft and milder than black or white peppercorns. Find them at your grocer on the same aisle as herbs and spices.

MENU IDEA FOR 6

• Red Beans and Rice
• Romaine salad
• French bread

GROCERIES NEEDED

Check staples: olive oil, garlic powder, butter, salad dressing

• 1 (1-lb.) package spicy or mild smoked turkey or pork sausage
• 1 large onion
• 4 (15-oz.) cans New Orleans-style red kidney beans (we tested with Van Camp's New Orleans Style)
• 1 small jar Cajun seasoning
• 2 (3.5-oz.) bags boil-in-bag brown rice
• 1 bunch green onions (optional)
• 1 (10-oz.) package romaine lettuce
• French bread

PER ENTRÉE SERVING:
CALORIES 507 (24% from fat); FAT 13.6g (sat 5.8g, mono 4.8g, poly 1.9g); PROTEIN 27.5g; CARB 74.2g; FIBER 16.2g; CHOL 50mg; IRON 11.9mg; SODIUM 1982mg; CALC 165mg

Prep: 5 min. ✳ **Cook:** 37 min.

Red Beans and Rice

Makes 6 servings

"I'm originally from Louisiana, so this sort of recipe is commonplace in my house. After a full day at school and gymnastics, my 6-year-old daughter is really hungry, and this fills her up!" —Suzanne O., Universal City, TX

1 Tbsp. olive oil
1 (1-lb.) package spicy or mild smoked turkey or pork sausage, cut into ¼-inch slices
1 large onion, finely chopped

4 (15-oz.) cans New Orleans-style red kidney beans, undrained
1 Tbsp. Cajun seasoning
2 tsp. garlic powder, divided

2 (3.5-oz.) bags boil-in-bag brown rice
2 Tbsp. butter or margarine
Sliced green onions (optional)

1. Heat olive oil in a Dutch oven over medium-high heat. Add sausage and onion; cook 7 minutes, stirring often. Remove from heat, and drain well. Return sausage mixture to Dutch oven; set aside.

2. Using a fork, mash 1 can beans in a small bowl. Add mashed beans and remaining 3 cans beans to sausage mixture. Stir in Cajun seasoning and 1 tsp. garlic powder; bring to a boil, reduce heat, and simmer, uncovered, 28 to 30 minutes, stirring occasionally.

3. Meanwhile, cook rice according to package directions; drain. Add remaining 1 tsp. garlic powder and butter, tossing gently until butter melts. Add rice mixture into bean mixture, stirring until combined. Sprinkle with sliced green onions, if desired.

Flavor Note: Amazingly, many kids, like Suzanne's, prefer spicy foods. For a mild version of this New Orleans favorite, scale back on the Cajun seasoning and offer bottled hot sauce at the table for those who want to kick up the heat.

MENU IDEA FOR 4

- Fresh Tortellini with Mushrooms and Pancetta

- Italian bread

- Lemon granita or Italian ice

GROCERIES NEEDED

Check staples: bottled minced garlic, pepper, shredded Parmesan cheese

- 1 (9-oz.) package refrigerated cheese tortellini (we tested with DiGiorno)

- 3 oz. pancetta or bacon

- 1 (8-oz.) package sliced fresh mushrooms

- 1 small onion

- 2 cups baby spinach

- 1 (14-oz.) can chicken broth

- 1 jar dried tomato bits

- 1 loaf Italian bread

- 2 pt. lemon granita or Italian ice

PER ENTRÉE SERVING:
CALORIES 367 (32% from fat); FAT 13.2g (sat 5.6g, mono 0.5g, poly 0.3g); PROTEIN 17.1g; CARB 45g; FIBER 4.2g; CHOL 41mg; IRON 1.5mg; SODIUM 1101mg; CALC 100mg

Prep: 8 min. ❊ **Cook:** 12 min.

Fresh Tortellini with Mushrooms and Pancetta

Makes 4 servings

Think most kids don't care for mushrooms? Think again. Budding gourmets love this combination of sautéed mushrooms and cheesy tortellini. Serve it with Italian bread, and encourage everyone to soak up every drop of flavor.

1 (9-oz.) package refrigerated cheese tortellini

3 oz. pancetta or bacon, diced
1 (8-oz.) package sliced fresh mushrooms
1 small onion, chopped
1 tsp. bottled minced garlic
2 cups baby spinach
1 cup chicken broth
½ cup dried tomato bits
¼ tsp. pepper
¼ cup shredded Parmesan cheese

1. Cook pasta according to package directions; drain and place in a large bowl. Keep warm.

2. Meanwhile, heat a large skillet over medium-high heat; add pancetta. Cook 5 minutes or until almost crisp, stirring occasionally; drain. Add mushrooms, onion, and garlic; cook 4 minutes or until onion is tender, stirring often. Add spinach, broth, tomato bits, and pepper. Cook 2 minutes or until spinach wilts, stirring often. Add to pasta, tossing to combine. Divide pasta mixture evenly among 4 bowls. Sprinkle with cheese.

Substitution Note: Pancetta is an Italian bacon cured with salt and spices. If you make the switch to use ordinary bacon, the recipe will look the same but it'll have a mild smoky flavor.

MENU IDEA FOR 4

- Chicken with Dried Tomato Sauce
- Basmati rice
- Steamed green beans

GROCERIES NEEDED

Check staples: salt, pepper, dried oregano, balsamic vinegar

- 1 (8-oz.) jar dried tomatoes in oil
- 4 (6-oz.) skinned and boned chicken breasts
- 1 (14-oz.) can chicken broth
- 1 bunch fresh oregano (optional)
- 1 package basmati rice
- 1 lb. fresh or frozen green beans

PER ENTRÉE SERVING:
CALORIES 219 (16% from fat); FAT 4g (sat 0.7g, mono 1.3g, poly 0.7g); PROTEIN 40.3g; CARB 3.1g; FIBER 0.7g; CHOL 101mg; IRON 1.7mg; SODIUM 666mg; CALC 30mg

Prep: 14 min. ❄ **Cook:** 16 min.

Chicken with Dried Tomato Sauce

Makes 4 servings

Balsamic vinegar and dried tomatoes give this simple chicken dish sophisticated flavor. If one of your kids cleans his or her plate, you may have a future chef on your hands.

1 (8-oz.) jar dried tomatoes in oil

4 (6-oz.) skinned and boned chicken breasts
¼ tsp. salt, divided
¼ tsp. pepper

1 cup chicken broth
1 tsp. dried oregano
½ tsp. balsamic vinegar
Garnish: fresh oregano sprig

1. Drain 1½ Tbsp. oil from jar of tomatoes into a large skillet; set aside. Remove ¼ cup dried tomatoes from jar, and finely chop. Refrigerate remaining tomatoes and oil in jar for another use.

2. Place chicken between 2 sheets of heavy-duty plastic wrap, and flatten to ½-inch thickness, using a meat mallet or rolling pin. Sprinkle chicken with ⅛ tsp. salt and pepper.

3. Heat 1½ Tbsp. reserved oil in large skillet over medium heat until hot. Add chicken; cook 6 minutes on each side or until done. Remove chicken from pan; keep warm.

4. Add chopped dried tomatoes, remaining ⅛ tsp. salt, chicken broth, oregano, and vinegar to pan; bring to a boil, scraping to loosen browned bits from pan. Cook 3 minutes or until broth mixture is reduced to about ½ cup. Serve sauce over chicken. Garnish, if desired.

278

MENU IDEA FOR 4

- Calypso Chicken
- Broccoli florets with Ranch dressing

GROCERIES NEEDED

Check staples: all-purpose flour, Ranch dressing

- 1 large oven cooking bag
- 1 (15-oz.) can pineapple chunks in juice
- 1 (8-oz.) package black bean-rice mix (we tested with Zatarain's)
- 1 (10½-oz.) can chicken broth
- 1 bunch fresh cilantro
- 4 (8-oz.) bone-in chicken breasts
- 2 broccoli crowns or 1 bag broccoli florets

PER ENTRÉE SERVING:
CALORIES 442 (7% from fat); FAT 3.5g (sat 0.7g, mono 0.5g, poly 0.5g); PROTEIN 43.4g; CARB 58.3g; FIBER 5.1g; CHOL 89mg; IRON 3.1mg; SODIUM 1233mg; CALC 91mg

Prep: 10 min. ✳ **Cook:** 45 min.

Calypso Chicken

Makes 4 servings

Some youngsters found the mingling of sweet and savory flavors in this island-inspired dish delicious. If you have some that don't, it's easy to serve the chicken with the black bean-rice mix on the side.

1 large oven cooking bag
1 Tbsp. all-purpose flour

1 (15-oz.) can pineapple chunks in juice, undrained
1 (8-oz.) package black bean-rice mix
1 (10½-oz.) can chicken broth
½ cup water
1 Tbsp. chopped fresh cilantro

4 (8-oz.) bone-in chicken breasts, skinned

1. Preheat oven to 350°. Place oven cooking bag in a 13- x 9-inch baking dish. Add flour to bag; twist end of oven bag, and shake to distribute.

2. Add pineapple and next 4 ingredients to oven bag, and squeeze bag to blend ingredients.

3. Arrange chicken in an even layer over rice mixture. Close oven bag with nylon tie; cut 6 (½-inch) slits in top of bag. Bake at 350° for 40 to 45 minutes or until chicken is done.

Preparation and Serving Note: Kimberly B., of Charlotte, NC, is a fan of oven cooking bags because the meats are juicy and cleanup is a cinch. She prefers using boneless chicken breasts in this recipe because they're easier to cut up for small children.

MENU IDEA FOR 4

• Pasta with Beans and Greens

• Vanilla ice cream with chocolate syrup

GROCERIES NEEDED

Check staples: olive oil, bottled minced garlic, salt, pepper, shredded Parmesan cheese

• 8 oz. uncooked bow tie pasta

• 1 large onion

• 1 (8-oz.) package sliced fresh mushrooms

• 1 (6-oz.) bag fresh spinach or kale

• 1 (14-oz.) can chicken broth

• 1 (15-oz.) can great Northern beans

• ¹/₂ gal. vanilla ice cream

• 1 bottle chocolate syrup

PER ENTRÉE SERVING:
CALORIES 332 (15% from fat);
FAT 5.4g (sat 1.5g, mono 2.1g,
poly 0.4g); PROTEIN 16.1g;
CARB 58.6g; FIBER 6.6g; CHOL 6mg;
IRON 3.9mg; SODIUM 1909mg;
CALC 134mg

Prep: 20 min. ❊ **Cook:** 16 min.

Pasta with Beans and Greens

Makes 4 servings

This meatless main dish boasts generous amounts of protein, fiber, complex carbohydrates, iron, and calcium. So, splurge a little on dessert.

8 oz. uncooked bow tie pasta

1 large onion, chopped
1 (8-oz.) package sliced fresh mushrooms
2 tsp. olive oil

4 cups chopped fresh spinach or kale (about 6 oz.)
1 cup chicken broth
1 tsp. bottled minced garlic
¹/₂ tsp. salt
¹/₂ tsp. pepper
1 (15-oz.) can great Northern beans, drained and rinsed

¹/₄ cup shredded Parmesan cheese

1. Cook pasta according to package direction; drain. Place pasta in a large bowl; set aside.

2. Meanwhile, sauté onion and mushrooms in hot oil in a large skillet over medium heat 5 minutes. Add spinach and next 4 ingredients; cook, stirring often, 10 minutes or until spinach is tender. Stir in beans, and cook 1 minute.

3. Add bean mixture to pasta; toss gently. Sprinkle with cheese. Serve immediately.

MENU IDEA FOR 4

- Sausage and Apple Stuffed Pork Chops
- Mashed potatoes
- Brussels sprouts

GROCERIES NEEDED

Check staples: butter, soft breadcrumbs, salt, pepper, vegetable cooking spray, cornstarch

- ¹/₄ lb. ground pork sausage
- 1 small Granny Smith apple
- 1 small onion
- 4 (8-oz.) bone-in pork chops (about ³/₄ inch thick)
- 1 cup apple juice
- 1 (24-oz.) package refrigerated mashed potatoes
- 1 lb. fresh Brussels sprouts or 1 (10-oz.) package frozen Brussels sprouts

PER ENTRÉE SERVING:
CALORIES 483 (50% from fat); FAT 26.8g (sat 10.3g, mono 11.4g, poly 2.5g); PROTEIN 40.7g; CARB 18.2g; FIBER 1.3g; CHOL 130mg; IRON 1.9mg; SODIUM 459mg; CALC 62mg

Prep: 20 min. ✳ **Cook:** 31 min.

Sausage and Apple Stuffed Pork Chops

Makes 4 servings

Lots of kids won't hesitate digging into this hearty portion size that includes plenty of gravy for the mashed potatoes.

¹/₄ lb. ground pork sausage
1 Tbsp. butter or margarine
1 small Granny Smith apple, cored and finely chopped
¹/₂ small onion, finely chopped
¹/₂ cup soft breadcrumbs

4 (8-oz.) bone-in pork chops (about ³/₄ inch thick)
¹/₄ tsp. salt
¹/₄ tsp. pepper
Vegetable cooking spray

1 cup apple juice
2 tsp. cornstarch

1. Cook sausage in a large skillet over medium-high heat, stirring until it crumbles and is no longer pink. Drain and pat dry with paper towels. Wipe skillet clean. Melt butter in same skillet over medium-high heat; add apple and onion; sauté 3 minutes or until crisp-tender. Stir in sausage and breadcrumbs. (Mixture will be slightly dry.) Set aside.

2. Trim excess fat from each chop. Cut a deep slit in 1 side of each chop to form a pocket. Pack stuffing evenly into each pocket. Sprinkle with salt and pepper. Coat both sides of chops with cooking spray.

3. Place same skillet over medium-high heat until hot. Add stuffed chops. Cook 8 minutes on each side or until done. Remove chops from pan; keep warm.

4. Whisk together apple juice and cornstarch in skillet. Bring to a boil over medium heat, stirring constantly, 1 minute. Return chops to pan; cover and simmer 1 more minute.

index